Introductory Visual Basic.NET

P. K. McBride

THOMSON

Australia • Canada • Mexico • Singapore • Spain • United Kingdom • United States

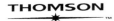

Introductory Visual Basic.NET
Copyright © P. K. McBride 2005

The Thomson logo is a registered trademark used herein under licence.

For more information contact Thomson Learning, High Holborn House, 50–51 Bedford Row, London
WC1 4LR or visit us on the World Wide Web at: http://www.thomsonlearning.co.uk

British Library Cataloguing-in-Publication Data

A catalogue record for this book is available from the British Library.

ISBN 1-8448-0190-X
First Edition published 2005 by Thomson Learning

Typeset by P. K. McBride, Southampton
Printed and bound in Great Britain by TJ International, Padstow, Cornwall

Disclaimer

The programs presented in this book have been included for their instructional value. They have been tested with considerable care, but are not guaranteed for any particular purpose. The author and the publisher do not offer any warranties or representations, nor do they accept any liabilities with respect to the programs.

Contents

Preface

Aim and need

For some years, Microsoft Windows has been the standard operating environment for PCs, and Visual Basic has become the standard programming language for Windows. As a result, many employers are demanding that computing students are familiar with Visual Basic, and many courses from NVQ to degree level include a Visual Basic component. This book has been specially written for these students, some of whom may have had some programming experience, to provide a concise and practical introductory-level text on Visual Basic.

Approach

The book introduces the concepts and techniques of Visual Basic across a broad front. It then goes deeper into key aspects of the system, bringing in new objects and language elements as they are needed, and using larger (and more interesting) example programs for illustration.

Where appropriate, there are short in-text programming tasks to give immediate practice in the techniques the text is introducing. At the end of most chapters, there are longer programming exercises. Some of these have sample answers at the end of the book, others are either too trivial or have too many possible solutions for any one to be held up as the 'correct' answer.

An introduction to Visual Basic.NET

Visual Basic is the language that many developers, including Microsoft, use to write new applications software. At the last count there were well over a million Visual Basic applications in commercial use! Look closely at any Windows database, spreadsheet or word processing package, whether from Microsoft or any other software house, and you will find that its macro language is either a variety of Visual Basic, or almost identical to it. For this reason, anyone who wants to become a Windows expert should master this language, and all Windows users, beyond the most casual, should have a grasp of it.

Visual Basic is substantially different from traditional programming languages. With these you could develop a program line by line, testing each command as you write it. (It's not the most efficient way to write software, but it works.) You could also take the same linear approach to learning the language, mastering one command at a time, and steadily building your knowledge. With Visual Basic you must develop your programs and your understanding across a broader front. You write a program by assembling the objects that you will use for screen displays and interaction with the users, adjusting the properties of those objects, determining which events they will respond to, thinking through the variables you need for holding data and for passing information from one part of the program to another, and writing the command lines that will run when events are activated. At each stage of development, you may add to or change any aspect of the program, but it must be done with an awareness of how it will affect the other aspects. Objects, properties, events and code are all interwoven. I have tried to take this same broad front approach in writing this book.

Visual Basic has been evolving steadily, with each new version offering more features. The current version, Visual Basic.NET, is a highly sophisticated language, which can be used to create ActiveX applets for Web pages or WAP-enabled mobiles, as well as free-standing applications. It is fully compatible with the other languages in Microsoft's Visual Studio set, and its programs can share data and functions with programs written in any other .NET language.

This is an introductory book. Its aim is to help you master the core concepts and techniques, and to give the reader the confidence to go on afterwards to explore the many possiblities of this rich and complex language.

P. K. McBride
Summer 2004

1 Visual Basic concepts

The concepts, techniques and tools for programming in Visual Basic are so interrelated that you need to understand how they fit together before you can really get to grips with any single area. This chapter lays a broad foundation on which to build your understanding of the language.

1.1 Event-driven programming

Traditional programming is essentially linear and based on the flow of execution. Operations run for a fixed span or until they reach decision points written into the program, and interrupting an on-going activity is either difficult or impossible to manage. Programmers are responsible for all aspects of their program, including the screen display and user interface, and must write the code to do everything. If they want particularly elegant screen effects, then they have got their work cut out. Programs are usually designed from top down, perhaps following the Jackson Structured Programming method, by decomposing complex operations into successively simpler ones. Sometimes a modular approach will be taken, creating a program from a set of more-or-less self-contained functions and procedures. In theory this makes it possible to reuse modules – perhaps those that produce the fancy screen effects – in other programs. In practice, there are generally very few routines that can be reused without major reworking.

Object-oriented programming

Visual Basic is *object-oriented* (OO), i.e. it revolves around ready-made objects, and it is *event-driven*, i.e. all the activities in a program are triggered by one event or another. Each object has its own *properties*, determining its position, size, colour, the appearance and nature of its text, and much more. Each object also has its own *event-handling methods*. The Visual Basic system knows all about these already. It knows what a Button is and how it works. It also knows how to handle images, menus, toolbars, dialog boxes and much else.

The programmer's job is to determine where, how and when an object appears on screen, what its text reads, and what happens when an event occurs. That event might be the opening of a form, the user clicking on a Button or typing text into a box. The programmer does not have to write code to trap these events – the system does that automatically. Because the program code runs in response to events, and as at any point a whole range of events might be possible, the flow of execution is not as fixed as in a traditional program. Operations do not have to follow a set sequence and can be easily interrupted, suspended or abandoned.

The process of program design reflects the nature of the system. You begin by creating the screen layout (the user-interface in the jargon), and work outwards from here, adding first the code that will run in response to specific events and then any necessary code to co-ordinate the whole program.

The nature of objects

To understand the characteristics of objects, let's take a real world analogy. Think of a car. It has certain characteristics including its shape, colour, and speed and direction (when moving). In OO jargon, these are *properties*, which may be set at the time of creation and/or during the program's execution. It can also do things, and have things done to it, such as opening and closing doors, driving, turning, braking and/or crashing. An object's activities are controlled by *methods* – blocks of code. Some methods may be fully written already, so that you can simply utilise what's there to do a job. Some methods are little more than shells, containing only the code to link them to an event or property – it's then up to you to write the code for the activity. You can also rewrite or *override* the code of a fully written method if you need to modify its activity.

Where do objects come from? Let's go back to the car analogy. Cars are created to the pattern defined in a blueprint (actually, nowadays it will be a set of CAD files, but just bear with me on this) and you can produce as many as you need from the same blueprint. In OO programming, *classes* are the blueprints for objects. The car analogy breaks down a bit here, as both the class and the object are blocks of data and methods. The difference is that, for any single class, there can be any number of objects derived from it, or *instances* of it, to use the OO jargon.

An object takes on, or *inherits*, all the characteristics and code of its class, but you can change or add to them. You can define new classes of your own based on existing classes, and – as with objects – the new ones inherit the characteristics of the base class.

There's a lot more to object-oriented programming theory than this, but we'll come back to it as and when we need it. This is a practical book.

The .Net Framework

Like all the current generation of Microsoft languages, Visual Basic can be used to create Web applications within the .Net Framework. Amongst other things, this offers a common runtime environment (whichever language is used), access to data held in standard structures and the use of XML services. The big advantage of .Net to programmers is that it allows them to produce applications for the Internet without having to learn a new language.

1.2   Terminology

Form

The form is the central unit in Visual Basic. It is a window, initially blank, on which you paste *controls* (see below) to create your screen or printer display. The form can be any size or colour, and you can attach to it code that will run when the form is loaded, closed or when the mouse is clicked or moves over it. A simple program may use only one form, others may have several forms, each of which will handle a different part of the program. One form may be for getting input from the user, a second for displaying results on the screen, a third for sending output to the printer. The forms may exist independently, or be displayed within a *parent* form.

Controls

These are the objects which can be pasted onto a form and range from Labels which display text, through PictureBoxes for images, to Buttons, CheckBoxes, Menus and Toolbars, to standard dialog boxes. Their properties, and the events they can handle, vary to suit their nature. Each control can have code attached to it – though not all will have. A Label or a PictureBox, for example, may well be there simply to improve the display, and not as the startpoint for any activities.

Subroutine

The code in a program is mainly written in subroutines or *subs* for short. Most of these will be attached to a control, but some are free-standing blocks of code. All subroutines start with the keyword `Sub` and close with `End Sub`.

Function

A function is a block of code which calculates a value. Visual Basic comes equipped with a large bank of ready-made functions for manipulating text, numbers and other values. You can create your own functions as required.

Module

Code that is attached to a form is accessible from anywhere on that form, but a program may have more than one form. It will sometimes be necessary to have code that can be reached from any form, and in this case the code would be written in a module. Modules disappear from view when the program runs – only forms have an on-screen existence. There may be several modules in one program.

Project

A project is a collection of forms and modules that make up a program – or part of a program (see *Solution*). When you want to start work on a program, you only have to open the one project file rather than a whole set of forms and modules.

Solution

Every program has a solution file, which serves to organise its components, but if required, several projects can be collected into a solution, to create a single program. These projects may be written in any of the .Net languages.

1.3   Visual Studio

Visual Studio is the development environment, the window where you design, build and debug your programs. In its window, you have everything that you need for producing programs – apart from your own ingenuity and creativity. The ready-made screen elements and other objects are all at hand, ready to be dragged and dropped into place; options, properties and methods are all listed and can usually be set or selected with a couple of clicks. As Visual Basic is a large system, it makes life much easier to have its many features so accessible, but note that the Studio can also be used with other Microsoft programming languages, such as Visual Java and Visual C#. This has obvious advantages for programmers who work in several languages, but it does add to the size and complexity of the Studio environment.

Starting work

TheVisual Studio has a multiple window display. This works best on a large screen – the one in Figure 1.1 has been shrunk to fit on the page! Notice the Dynamic Help

Figure 1.1

Visual Studio

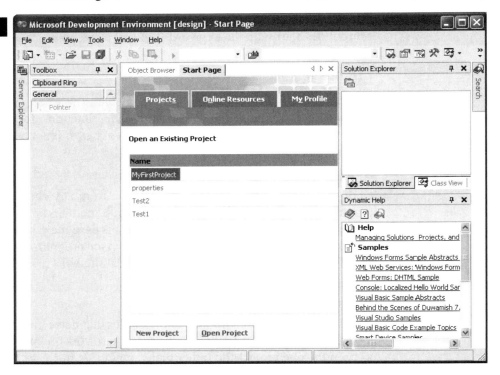

window at the bottom right – the topics listed here reflect what you are doing at the time. When the Studio first opens, you are presented with the Start Page. This has three tabs, **Projects**, **Online Resources** and **My Profile**.

My Profile

Projects is the tab that you would normally use at start up, but when you are in Visual Studio for the very first time, you should go to **My Profile** so that you can customise the Studio.

To set up Visual Studio for your work:

1 At the **Start Page**, click on the **My Profile** tab.
2 Drop-down the **Profile** list and select *Visual Basic Developer*.
3 Check that the other boxes are also set to *Visual Basic*.
4 Help can be displayed within Visual Studio (Internal) or in its own window (External) – click a radio Button to set your preference.
♦ If you change the **Show Help** option, your PC will think very hard for several minutes while it reorganises its Help files. Just wait for the update to finish.

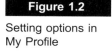

Figure 1.2

Setting options in My Profile

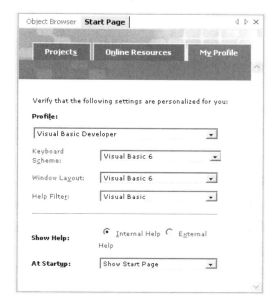

Opening a project

If the sample files have been installed, you can use them to practise opening projects. They demonstrate a variety of programming techniques – though the code may not make much sense until you have a reasonable grasp of the language. Open a project so that you can see what the screen looks like when the Studio is in use.

1 Click **Open Project**.

2   At the **Open Project** dialog box, go to the **Look in** folder. To reach the sample, you probably need to work down through **Program Files > Visual Studio > VB > VB Samples** (or something similar, depending on your setup).

3   Each project is stored in its own folder. Open the folder. You should find a file with an *.sln* (VB Solution) extension, and possibly one with a *.vbproj* extension. Select either of those and click **Open**.

◆   If the project has been used recently, it will be listed on the Start Page – simply click on the name to start.

4   At first, the central window will probably be empty. Look in the Solution Explorer (at the top right) for a file with a *.vb* extension. Double-click on this to open the project's form in the central window.

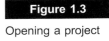

Figure 1.3

Opening a project

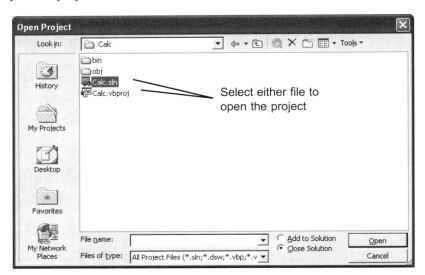

1.4   Arranging the Visual Studio

When you are working on a program in Visual Basic, the screen will look something like that shown in Figure 1.4. Only the Menu bar and the central Design and coding window are fixed. All the other components can be moved, resized or closed if not needed. It means that you can tailor your screen to suit your own way of working and the job in hand, but it also means that your screen is unlikely to look exactly the same as the screenshots in this book.

The Studio's screen display is infinitely flexible. You can open and close windows, resize them, lay them one on top of another, or set them floating anywhere on – or off – the Studio area.

Moving windows

A window can be moved by dragging on its title bar, or on its tab if it shares an area with another window. While you are dragging, it is shown as an outline and the

Figure 1.4

The working screen
— as most of the
elements can be
moved, resized or
hidden, yours may
not look like this

Click on the name to open the set of tools

Form design and coding area

Solution Explorer

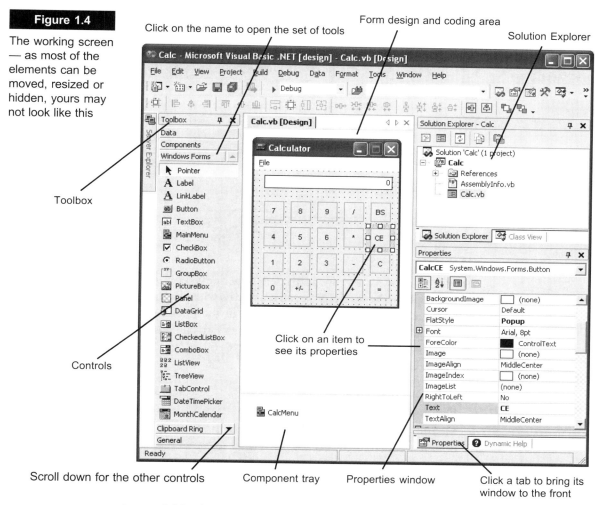

Toolbox

Controls

Click on an item to
see its properties

Scroll down for the other controls

Component tray

Properties window

Click a tab to bring its
window to the front

shape of this shows how the window will fit into the display when you release it.
A window can be docked – fixed flush up against the frame – at the top, bottom,
left or right of the Studio window. When the outline is in a docking area, it will align
to the frame, showing you how it will fit.

If the docking area already has a window in it, the new window can share the
space in three ways:

- Tiled one above the other, and sharing the space. The new one will go on top.
- Tiled side by side.
- Layered, one over the other, with a tab at the bottom for switching between
  them. When the outline is in the right place for layering, the tab will appear.

If a window is already layered, dragging on the title bar moves the whole set of
layered windows. Drag on the tab if you just want to move the one window.

If the outline is a simple rectangle, and not aligned to any part of the main frame,
this will become a floating window.

Figure 1.5

Outlines seen when
moving windows
over other ones

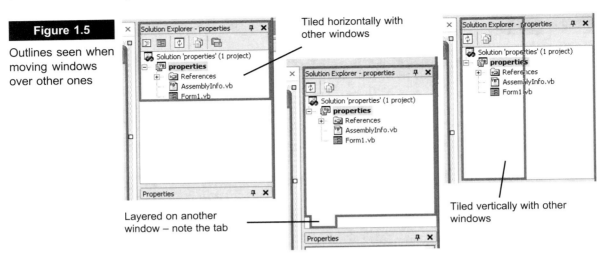

Tiled horizontally with
other windows

Layered on another
window – note the tab

Tiled vertically with other
windows

Changing the size

Docked windows are more restricted. One docked at the left or right will occupy
the full depth of the frame. You can change its width by dragging on its inner border.
If there are two or more windows tiled in the docking area, they will together
occupy the full depth and width of the area. You can change their relative sizes by
dragging on the boundary between them. If you drag on the inner border, it affects
the width of the whole docking area.

- Windows docked at the top and bottom of the screen behave similarly – only
  their depth can be changed.
- Floating windows can be resized freely. Point to any side or corner to get the
  double-headed arrow cursor, then drag to move the frame in or out.

Auto Hide

Auto Hide tucks windows out of the way when they are not in use. It is shown and
controlled by the pin on the right of the title bar.
- When the pin is upright ╬ Auto Hide is off and the window stays open. Click
  the pin to turn Auto Hide on.
- When the pin is on its side ⊨ Auto Hide is on and the window shrinks into the
  outer frame when not in use. To open a hidden window, point to its tab in the
  outer frame.

Opening and closing windows

If a window isn't needed, close it – click the **Close** Button ✕.

To reopen a window:
1 Open the **View** menu.
2 Click on the window to open.
Or

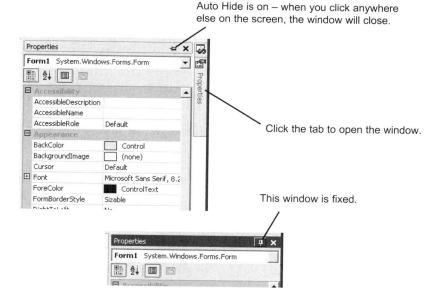

Figure 1.6

Turn on Auto Hide
for those windows
that you rarely use

Auto Hide is on – when you click anywhere
else on the screen, the window will close.

Click the tab to open the window.

This window is fixed.

♦ Use the keyboard shortcuts – they are listed on the **View** menu.

Or

♦ Click the Buttons in the Standard toolbar to open the Properties 🗗 or Toolbox
🛠 windows.

To restore the default display:

1 Go to the Start Page and open the **My Profile** tab.
2 Select *Visual Basic 6* as the Window Layout.
3 Click the **Design** Button at the top of the central area to return to the Design
window and display the form.

Task 1.1

Get Visual Basic up and running and identify the component windows. If
any are not present, open them from the View menu.

1.5   The Toolbox

This holds five sets of controls. The one that we will be mainly using is the
Windows Forms set which has all the standard Windows facilities, such as
Buttons, scroll bars and dialog boxes, as well as text, image and drawing tools.
There are a lot of them! Even with the Studio window maximised on a high-
resolution screen, there will still be around a dozen that you cannot see (the image
in Figure 1.7 is a collage). Fortunately, those that you are likely to need regularly
are clustered towards the top.

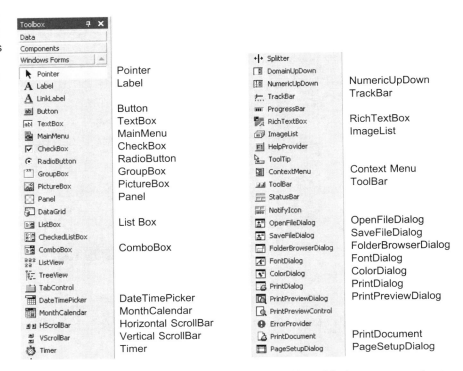

Figure 1.7

The Windows Forms set of controls – the labelled ones will all be used at some point in this book

To reach the other controls, scroll through the list with the arrows at the top and bottom of the display.

- The **Pointer** is used for selecting objects that have been placed on the form. The system reverts to this when you have finished using any other tool.

Most of the control tools are used in a similar way. When one is selected, a crosshair cursor appears. Place this on the form and drag to create an outline where the control is to go. If you get the initial position or size wrong, it can be adjusted later with the Pointer.

- **Labels**, **TextBoxes**, and **RichTextBoxes** all hold text, but the Label can only display and not receive input from the user. A simple TextBox can only handle plain text – though you can use any size or type of font. A RichTextBox can take fully formatted text and embedded images.

- **Button**s are one method of selection or starting operations. They are typically used where there are only a limited number of options – the choice may be OK or Cancel, Start or Quit.

- Add a **MainMenu** or a **ContextMenu** to a form when you want to create a menu structure on the main Menu bar, or one which opens when you right-click on an object. Both are create in similar ways (see page 64).

- A **CheckBox** acts as a toggle switch, turning an option on or off.

- **RadioButtons** are normally used to select one from a set of mutually exclusive options. At any one time there can only be one set on a form, unless they are enclosed in a GroupBox or Panel.

- **GroupBoxes** and **Panels** are both simply containers for group of controls The difference between them is that a GroupBox has a caption, but a Panel can have a vertical scroll bar if necessary. You must use one or other if you have several sets of RadioButtons on a form, but they can also be used just for convenience. The controls can all be moved around as a unit, and the frame is a visual reminder to the user that the controls are related in some way.

- A **Picture Box** holds pictures created with Paint or similar art packages. These must be in an acceptable format – .bmp, .wmf, .jpg, .gif, .ico or .dib.

- **List Boxes** display lists of items, so that the user can see what is available and select one. If the list is too long to fit in the box, vertical scroll bars will be added at runtime. Items can only be added to the list during run-time, not at design time.

- A **ComboBox** combines a drop-down list with a text box in which users can enter their own data when the program is running.

- The **DateTime Picker** and **MonthCalendar** offer simple ways for the user to set the date or time.

- The **Horizontal** and **Vertical ScrollBar**s are used on forms to give a very flexible way to set values. You set the minimum and maximum values and the change produced by large and small movements of the slider. When the program is running, the position of the slider determines the value returned by the scroll bar.

- The **NumericUpDown** and **TrackBar** are variations on the ScrollBars. This NumericUpDown is, in effect, a TextBox with a squashed VScrollBar on the side. Values can be typed directly into the box, or changed by clicking the up/ down arrows.The TrackBar has a marked scale, and the slider hops from one tick to another, instead of the smooth continuous change of a ScrollBar.

- The **Timer** is unusual in that it is invisible once the program is running. Its purpose is to control actions that must take place at or after set intervals. You could use one to set a time limit for a response to a question, or to produce a ticking clock.

- The main use of an **ImageList** is to hold the icons to be displayed on a Toolbar.

- A **Toolbar** fits in the top area of a form, beneath the Menu Bar (if present). The tools that you create on it will be text-only unless you link in an ImageList.

- The **OpenFileDialog**, **SaveFileDialog**, **FolderBrowserDialog**, **FontDialog** and **ColorDialog** produce the standard Windows dialog boxes for managing files and fonts. When these are placed on a form, they go into the Component tray at the bottom of the window. They appear on screen when called up from within the code (see Chapter 6).

- The **PrintDialog**, **PrintPreviewDialog** and **PageSetupDialog** are used for controlling printing. The output is first assembled in a **PrintDocument**.

Task 1.2

Use the Toolbox to place some controls on your form. Include a Label and a Command Button, as these will be wanted later in this section. Delete everything but the Label and the Button by first clicking on them, then pressing [Delete]. Adjust the size and position of your two objects with the Pointer, so that you have a layout something like that in Figure 1.8.

Figure 1.8

The first job in creating a program is to put the controls on the form

To move a control click anywhere on it and drag to its new position

To resize a control click on it to get the handles, then drag on a handle to pull an edge or corner in or out

Scroll down to reach the other controls

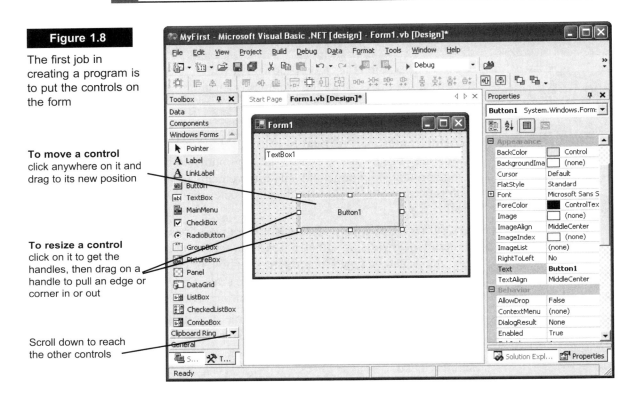

1.6 The Properties window

This is where you set the properties of objects. To do this:

1 Click on the control, or select its name from the drop-down list at the top of the Properties window.

2 Select the property to be set from the list. The properties vary with the nature of the control, but there are always those that cover its visible features and some aspects of its interaction with the rest of the system.

The properties are organised into headed groups. These can be collapsed if not wanted, so that you have easier access to those that you do use.

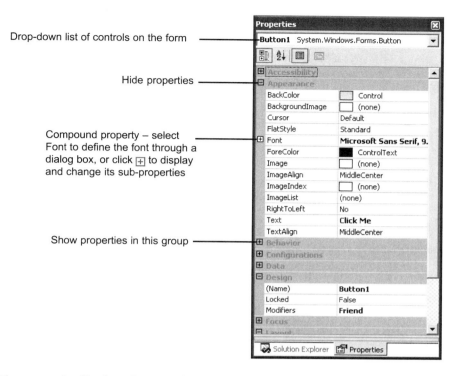

Figure 1.9

The Properties
window for a button

Drop-down list of controls on the form

Hide properties

Compound property – select
Font to define the font through a
dialog box, or click ⊞ to display
and change its sub-properties

Show properties in this group

The properties list for a Button, shown in Figure 1.9, includes:

- **Text** – the text that is written inside it;
- **Font** specifications – typeface, size and styles;
- **Colors** – for the Forecolor (ink) and the Background.
- **Name** – edit this to change the default names of *Button1*, *Button2*, etc. to something meaningful. As programs get more complex, memorable names become more useful. The text for the Text and Name can be edited with the normal Windows editing techniques.

Setting properties

New values can be typed directly into the property slot, or chosen from a set of options.

- Most options are given in *drop-down lists*, indicated by ▼ (this appears when the property is selected). Some of these lists are simply a choice of *True* or *False* to turn an effect on or off; others are more extensive.

- Where text or an image can be aligned vertically and horizontally, the options are selected from a graphic display. Click on the area where you want the item to be placed.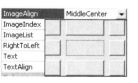

Colours

Colours are selected from a palette, also indicated by ▾. The choice is infinite – you have three different palettes to choose from, and you can define your own if nothing else suits. The three palettes are:

- **System** holds the colours that are used by Windows for the screen elements. If you use these, when the program is run on a PC with a different colour scheme, your colours will change to match the appropriate element of that scheme.

- The **Web** colours are those which can be displayed by browsers. If you are developing a Web application, you should restrict yourself to this set.

- **Custom** is the most flexible. It has a set of 48 predefined colours, and another 16 which you can define for yourself.

Figure 1.10

The colour palettes

Custom colours are labelled with their RGB (Red, Green, Blue) values

Use System colours if you want your colours to match the Windows colour scheme your users' PCs.

48 predefined colours

16 custom colours

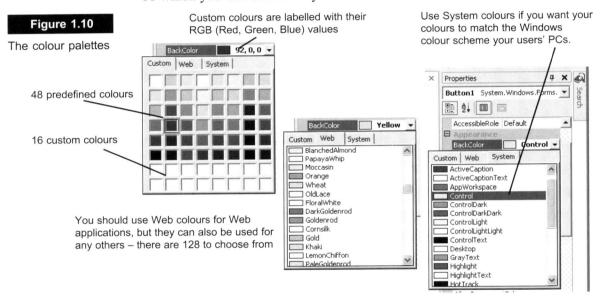

You should use Web colours for Web applications, but they can also be used for any others – there are 128 to choose from

Font

You can define all aspects of a font in one operation, through the standard Font dialog box, or define them separately.

To use the Font dialog box:

1 Select **Font** and click the ... Button.

2 Select the font, style and size, checking the appearance in the Sample slot.

3 Click **OK**.

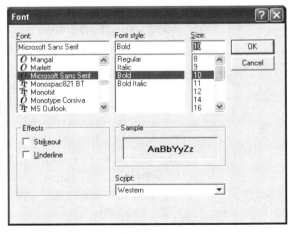

To set Font fields individually:

1 Click the ⊞ beside **Font** to open up the group.

2 To set the **Name**, select it from the list.

3 To set the **Size**, type a value. This is normally given in points, but you can set the **Units** to pixels, inches, millimetres or other units.

4 **Bold**, **Italic**, **Strikeout** and **Underline** are True/False values – select to turn effects on or off.

5 **GdiCharSet** and **GdiVerticalFont** refer to the graphical design interface system which gives more flexible ways of rendering fonts – and are best left to the specialists!

6 To set the colour of your text, use the **ForeColor** property.

⊟ Appearance	
BackColor	☐ Transparent
BackgroundImage	☐ (none)
Cursor	Default
FlatStyle	Standard
⊟ Font	**Comic Sans MS, 16pt**
Name	ab Comic Sans MS
Size	16
Unit	Point
Bold	False ▾
GdiCharSet	True
GdiVerticalFont	False
Italic	False
Strikeout	False
Underline	False
ForeColor	■ ControlText

Task 1.3

Explore the properties of the form and of the controls on your screen.

Change the Label's:

Text to '*Pressure Tester*' – type in new text;

Font size to 18 – use the Font dialog box;

Fore and Back Colors to any others – select from the palettes.

Change the Button's **Caption**, to read '*Click Me*'.

1.7 Controls and events

Just as each type of control has its own set of properties, some of which are common to all, so each also has its own set of events, and some of these are common to all controls. To get a flavour of what events are handled, place an object on the form and double-click on it. This opens the code window. It is here that you write the code to be attached to events.

Each event has its own method, or subroutine, and the opening and closing lines of these are already written for you. The name, in the opening line, is composed of the names of the control and the event, linked by an underscore. `Private` at the start means that the sub can only be accessed from controls on the same form. If you want to be able to activate the code from other forms this should be changed to `Public`.

There is always a set of () brackets at the end of the name, and enclosed in here will be the names and definitions of the parameters that are used to carry information from the event through to your code. With a TextBox's KeyPress event, for example, the opening line of the sub reads:

```
Private Sub TextBox1_KeyPress(ByVal sender As Object, ByVal e As
System.Windows.Forms.KeyPressEventArgs) Handles TextBox1.KeyPress
```

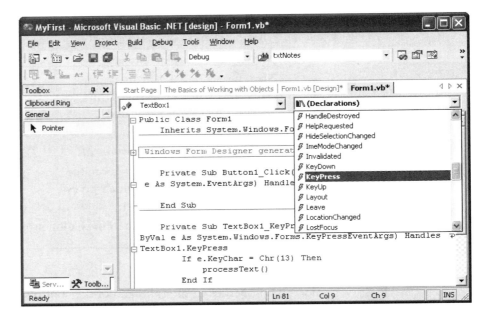

Figure 1.11

The Methods list in the code window

When this event is triggered, *e* (the KeyPressEventArgs) will hold information about the key that was pressed. (*e* is a class, rather than a simple variable, and has the property *KeyChar* which is the ASCII code of the key.) The code might well check this to see if the user had pressed a specific key, or one from an acceptable range.

When the code window first opens, it will display the sub for the most common event for that type of control. For example, with a Button, you are always offered the Click event. If this is not the event you want to handle, then you can select another by dropping down the list. If an event is not in that list, then the control cannot respond to it.

Task 1.4

Explore the events of the controls on your form. Which ones crop up regularly? Which ones are specific to certain controls?

1.8 The Help system

The Visual Studio has a very extensive and comprehensive Help system – in fact, its size can be a problem. You may be offered so much Help that you may not know where to start!

There are four ways into the Help system: Dynamic Help, Contents, Index and Search. Each has its own window, and you can have any or all of them open at any time. Whichever you use, you will be taken to the same set of Help pages. These, and other aspects of Help can be reached through the Help menu.

Figure 1.12

The Help page may contain links to other Help pages. The icons at the top of the Dynamic Help window open the other Help windows.

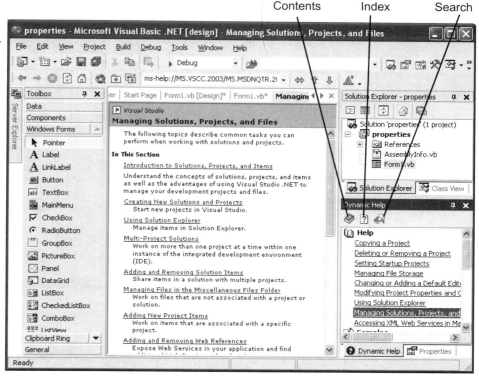

Dynamic Help

This reflects what you are doing at the time. When you first start, it will offer Help on the management of projects and similar getting-started topics. When you are laying out your forms, it will offer topics on the currently-selected control on a form; when you are writing code, it will offer Help on the methods and functions that you are using.

The Dynamic Help window is visible at the bottom right when you start. Once a project is opened, it will be overlaid by the Properties window.

1   To read a topic, click on its link. The Help page will be displayed in the central area of the screen.

2   The Help page may contain links to related or more detailed topics – click on the links to reach the Help you need.

3   When you have done with the Help, click on the appropriate tab at the top of the central area to get back to where you were.

Contents

This organises the Help pages into a 'book', with chapters and sub-sections within them. It's a good way into the Help system when you first start – as you can get a good overview of what is available; and it is also useful when you know more or less what you need Help on, but don't necessarily know the right words.

Open the chapters to see the subsection names and topic titles, and follow up any that sound promising. You may need to go down two or three levels to reach a Help page – and even that may be mainly a list of links to other pages.

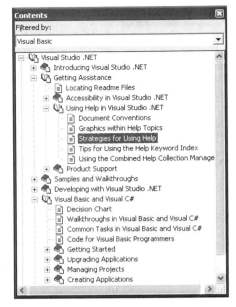

To use the contents:

1 Ensure that the **Filtered by** option is set to **Visual Basic** – so you only get the relevant Help pages!

2 Click ⊞ 🐦 to open a chapter or sub-section.

3 Click ⊟ 🦙 to close a set if there is nothing there that you want.

4 Click the topic title or 🗐 to open a Help page – it will be displayed in the central area.

Index

If you know the words for what you are looking for, you will find it faster through the Index than through the Contents. This has an alphabetical list of all the significant words in the Help system. Use it to find Help on specific controls, properties and methods.

1 Type in the first few letters of a word. The Index will scroll through to that part of the list.

2 Select the index entry.

3 The Index Results window will open at the bottom of the screen. Select a topic to display it in the central area.

4 Close the Index Results window when it is no longer needed.

Search

Use this as an alternative to the Index for finding Help on specific words. As a search finds every reference to the given word, it will normally produce more results than the Index, though a higher proportion will be less relevant. There are four search options:

- **Search in titles only** will find fewer results, but they will be more relevant.

- **Match related words** will find singulars and plurals of the same word, e.g. look for 'checkbox' and it will also find 'checkboxes'.

Figure 1.13

An index entry will typically produce many results, and some will be more relevant than others

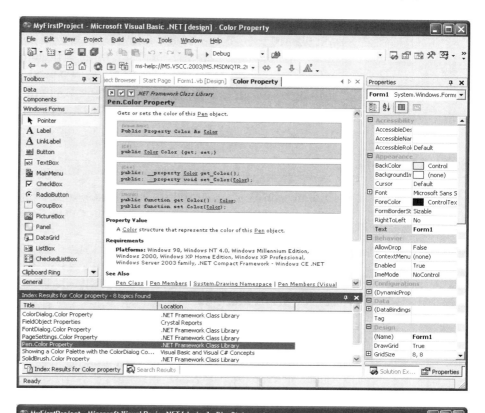

Figure 1.14

The Search Results window can list up to 500 topics – if you can't see what you need in the top few, redefine your search

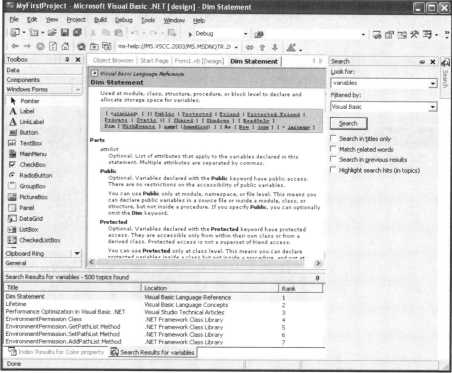

- **Search in previous results** allows you to run a search in several stages, e.g. if you wanted to read about MDI forms (multiple document interface) and windows, you could search first for 'MDI forms' (finding 78 pages), then search within those pages for 'windows' (finding 14 pages).

- **Highlight search hits (in topics)** puts a blue background on the search words in the Help pages.

1.9   Options

The Studio can be customised to your tastes. Some of the options are largely cosmetic – e.g. the fonts and colours that are used in the screen display – others have rather more impact on how you work.

Most should be left at their defaults until you have spent some time with the system. One or two are worth setting earlier on, and perhaps the most important is the projects location – the default folder for storing new projects.

To set the project location:

1   Open the **Tools** menu and select **Options…**

2   In the **Environment** folder, select **Projects and Solutions**.

3   For the **Visual Basic projects location** either click **Browse…** and locate the folder, or type the path to it.

4   Click **OK**.

While you have the dialog box open, check that the options in the **International Settings** area are correct and also check that the **Keyboard** is set for Visual Basic.

You should also know about the **Line numbers** option. This can be found in the **All Languages – General** section of the **Text Editor** area. If it is switched on, line numbers are displayed beside the code. These can be useful for debugging and for navigating around long programs. (There is a **Go To** command in the **Edit** menu which will jump you to any given line number.)

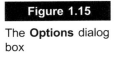

Figure 1.15

The **Options** dialog box

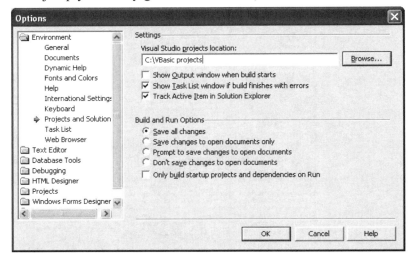

1.10   The programming language

Some words in the Visual Basic vocabulary will be familiar to those who have programmed in other languages; others arise from the Windows environment. The language has a very large vocabulary – there are around 400 keywords, statements, operators, methods, functions and properties that are specific to the Visual Basic library, and many thousands more in the wider Visual Studio set.

If you want to know what is there, open the **Help Contents**, select **Visual Studio .Net**, then **Visual Basic and Visual C#**, then **Reference** , then **Visual Basic Language** and start opening up the books within that to see the lists. Fortunately you do not have to learn them all! It is enough to know what is available, in general terms, as you can look up the exact word and its mode of use in the Help pages.

Types of words

The language can be divided into ten categories.

Constants

These are words which can be used in place of number values, making a program easier to read – and to write – as words are often more memorable than numbers. For example, in a routine to pick up a press on **[F1]** (key code 11) you could use the constant **vbKeyF1** instead of the number.

Data types

Define the nature of data and how it is to be stored and processed. There are two types of text, a dozen types of numbers, plus other simple and compound types of data. Visual Basic is normally tolerant about data types – allowing you to move data from one type of variable or object to another, even if part of the data may be lost in translation. (For example, copying data from a more complex number data type to a simpler one may reduce its level of accuracy.) You can force Visual Basic to accept only explicit conversion between types by writing **Option Strict On** at the very start of your code.

Functions

These take numbers, strings of text or other forms of data, perform an operation upon them and return a new value to the program. For example:

```
wordlen = Len(inputword)
```

Here **Len** calculates the length of the text in the variable *inputword*. If this had held "Dictionary", the resulting value of 10 would be passed back to the variable *wordlen*. Many of the functions will be familiar to those of you who have used traditional Basics, but – as with statements – some are specific to this system.

```
surname = InputBox ("Please enter your name")
```

The **InputBox** function arises from Windows. This line displays a standard dialog box, with your prompt, the usual **OK** and **Cancel** Buttons, and a text box in which to type data. In this example, whatever is typed is copied across to the variable *surname*.

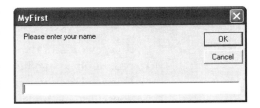

The function is used here in its simplest form. With a little extra effort you can add a title to the box, or a **?** or **!** symbol, or replace the **OK** with **Yes** and **No** Buttons.

Keywords

Keywords are mainly used for setting options in statements, e.g. the first line of a procedure usually reads:

```
Private Sub…
```

`Sub` is the statement which marks the start of the procedure; `Private` is the keyword that defines the access which other parts of the program can have to the code.

Statements

These are words that do things. Some you may recognise from other Basics, e.g.

```
ChDir D:\files\mydata
```

which **Ch**anges the **Dir**ectory.

```
For n = 1 To 10
    . . .
Next n
```

where the key words are `For ... To ... Next` that cause a set of commands to be executed a set number of times.

Others will be quite new. For instance:

```
MsgBox "Welcome to this program"
```

`MsgBox` generates a standard Windows message box with the usual OK Button. The text can be whatever you like – in this case it will display "Welcome to this program".

Methods

Like statements, these perform actions, but methods can only be used with suitable objects, e.g.:

```
PictureBox1.Hide()

TextBox1.Copy()
```

The first hides `PictureBox1`; the second copies into the Clipboard whatever text is selected in `TextBox1`. Different types of objects have different sets of methods that can be used with them. For example, you can only copy from objects in which you can select text.

Objects

The most important objects for us are the controls, but there are also other types of objects which do not necessarily have a screen presence. Whether you can see it or not, every object has a set of *properties* and *methods*.

Operators

These include the operators used in arithmetic and in logical expressions, and in comparisons.

Properties

These define the nature and appearance of objects. Properties can normally be set at design time – the Properties window being used to define those of controls – but can also be set during run time, either by the user or by the program.

Events

An event is an occurrence that the Visual Basic system can recognise and respond to. Events include users' actions, such as key presses and mouse movements, as well as changes to data or objects.

1.11 Attaching code

Where code is to be executed in response to an event, it is written into the sub that handles the event for that object. If you did Task 1.2, you should have a form containing a Label and a Button. That Button can handle, amongst other events, one called `Click`. We will add code so that when the Button is clicked, two messages appear on the screen. Each will be produced by a different type of code.

Figure 1.16

The Form window for the program – edit the Text and Font properties of the Label and button so that they are like the ones shown here

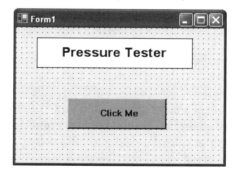

Double-click on the Button. The code window will appear, with the header line and an End Sub line which marks the end of the block. The cursor will be between them, ready for your code:

```
Private Sub Button1_Click(ByVal sender As Object, ByVal e As
System.EventArgs) Handles Button1.Click
    |
End Sub
```

You will notice that `Private Sub`, `End Sub` and some of the words inside the brackets are in blue. (This is the default colour, but it depends upon your setup.) Reserved words, which have a special meaning to the system, are shown in a different colour from other text.

Type in the following – and don't worry about capitals – the system will add these when it checks the lines, but note that there are no spaces within *Label1.Text*:

```
Label1.Text = "Ouch"
MsgBox("Don't click so hard")
```

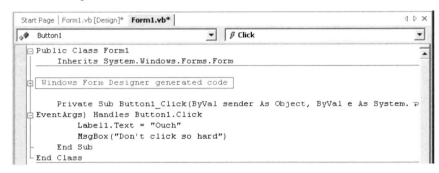

The Code window after adding the code

The first line is an example of changing the value of a property within a program. It assigns the text "Ouch" to the **Text** property of the **Label**. The second uses the `MsgBox` statement.

Run the program, by selecting **Debug | Start** or press **[F5]**. Click the Button and see what happens. Click it as often as you like. The code will continue to respond to the event as long as the program is running. To end the program, close its window, or select **Stop Debugging** from the **Debug** menu or click the ■ tool on the Debug toolbar (this will have appeared automatically).

To save the program for posterity, turn to the **File** menu and select **Save All**. The form and its project wil be saved using the file names and folder location that were all set up when you first started work.

1.12   Variables

A variable is a named space in memory where data can be stored. The values can be accessed and/or changed at any point during the program's execution.

Variables must be declared before they can be used. Declaration tells the VB compiler what name will be used and what kind of data is to be stored – and therefore how much space to allocate to it, and how to access the data.

To declare a variable, use the `Dim` statement, followed by the variable's name and type, in the form:

```
Dim variablename As datatype
```

The rules for **variable names** are simple:

- they must begin with a letter;

- they may contain any mixture of letters and numbers;

- they may not include punctuation or other symbols, with the exception of the under_score;
- they may not have more than 255 characters.

If you make the names meaningful, your code will be easier for you and others to read, and if you keep them short, you will reduce typing mistakes.

Data types

Visual Basic supports a wide range of data types. The simple data types are:

Short	whole numbers, in the range −32,768 to +32,767, held in 16 bits.
Integer	whole numbers in the range + or − 2 billion, held in 32 bits.
Long	64 bit whole numbers (ridiculously large).
Single	floating point numbers (i.e. with decimal fractions) held accurately to 7 digits.
Double	as Single, but held to 15 digit accuracy.
Decimal	numbers in the range +/− 8 * 10^{28}, held to 29 digit accuracy.
Char	single text character, stored in Unicode format.
String	variable length block of text of Unicode characters.
Boolean	can hold only the values *True* or *False*, given directly or assigned from the result of a logical test (see Chapter X).
Date	dates and time, counted in 100 nanosecond units from the start of the Gregorian calendar, but held in a readable form, e.g. at the time of writing, the date value is #24/4/2004 11:14# (see Chapter X).
Object	a highly flexible form of storage that can take data of any type, either generated within the program or imported from another application.

There are also compound data types, including structures, classes and arrays (see below).

Examples of variable declarations:

```
Dim Surname As String

Dim Salary As Decimal

Dim x, y As Integer
```

Note: You can declare several variables of the same type in one `Dim` line.

Arrays

An array is a set of variables of the same type, which share the same name, but with an identifying index number or *subscript*. The purpose of arrays is simple – by changing the subscript, the same routine can work on any or every value within an array. This is one of the things that allows computers to process masses of data.

In Visual Basic variable arrays can be huge. They may have up to 60 dimensions, and a dimension may have up to 32,767 subscripts. However, this does not mean that you can have 60 dimensions, each with 32,767 subscripts – you will run out of memory long before this. The practical maximum number of elements in an array is several million – depending upon the type of variable and the capacity of your PC. Arrays should be declared with `Dim` in the general declarations area, or with `Redim` (see below) in a sub.

Examples of array declarations:

```
Dim Results(50) As Integer
```

This creates a one-dimensional array of 51 integers, numbered from 0 to 50.

```
Dim Employees(0..200) As String
```

This will hold 201 text items, each of any length (though there is a nominal limit of 2 billion characters!).

```
Dim Table(9,19) As Single
```

This array has two dimensions, which you could think of as 10 (0 to 9) columns and 20 (0 to 19) rows.

```
Dim OxoGrid(3,3,3) As Short
```

The could be the 'playing area' for a game of three-dimensional Noughts and Crosses, with 4 layers of 4 rows and 4 columns.

```
Dim clients() As String
Dim mainstore(,,) As Double
```

These two lines create arrays, but without specifying their sizes – you may not know this at the start of the program. The array will expand to take whatever data is alloted to it, or its size can be set later with the ReDim command.

Note that all subscript numbering starts from 0.

Scope and duration of variables

A variable's scope – the code within which it can be accessed – is normally restricted to the sub or module in which it was written. A variable declared with a `Dim` in a sub exists only within that sub and its value is lost when the sub ends. One declared at the top of a form – above and outside of any subs – can be read or changed from anywhere within that form, but not from other forms in the program. One declared in a basic module can be accessed from anywhere (see Chapter 10).

Static

Use this instead of `Dim` in a sub if you want the variable to retain its value when the sub ends, so that it is still there when the program flow returns to the sub. For example, you might have this code attached to a Button called *btnAdd*:

```
Private Sub btnAdd_Click(ByVal sender As Object, ByVal e As
System.EventArgs) Handles btnAdd.Click()
    Static TotalSoFar As Integer
    TotalSoFar = TotalSoFar + NextNumber
End Sub
```

If *TotalSoFar* had been set up with `Dim`, its value would have been reset to zero every time the Button was clicked. Using `Static`, we can keep a running total in *TotalSoFar*, adding to it each time *cmdAdd* is clicked.

ReDim

Use this to set up arrays if you want to be able to change their size during the execution of the program – the size might depend on how much data the user wanted to store. `Redim` is an active statement, to be used within a sub and not at the top of a form. Existing data is normally erased from the array. Example:

```
Redim Marks(StudentNo) As Integer
```

where *StudentNo* is a value collected from the user at an earlier point in the program.

1.13   Controls for data storage

It is important to note that the values stored in controls are accessible to other parts of a program, and can therefore be used as an alternative to variables. When the user types something into a TextBox, it is stored in the **Text** property. This can be used by code attached to the TextBox, or to any other control. The line:

```
Label1.Text = Text1.Text
```

would copy whatever was in the TextBox into the Label.

1.14   Number operators

When calculating with numbers, you can use these arithmetic operators:

$\wedge$		Exponentiation (power)
+	–	Plus and minus
\	Mod	Integer division and remainder
*	/	Multiply and divide

The integer division operators may be new to you. Integer division (\) gives the whole number of times that the number can be divided, and Mod gives the remainder. e.g.

```
22 \ 5 = 4          22 Mod 5 = 2

7 \ 3.2 = 2         7 Mod 3.2 = 0.6
```

The minus sign can also be used to mark a negative number.

If the expression contains more than one operator, the calculation follows the normal rules of precedence, i.e. the operators are processed in the order:

```
^  -  (negative)  *  /  \  Mod  +  -
```

For example:

```
answer = 2^2 + 4 * 6 / 3 - 1
```

First $\wedge$ exponentiation…

```
answer = 4 + 4 * 6 / 3 - 1
```

Next multiplication and division...

```
answer = 4 + 24 / 3 - 1
answer = 4 + 8 - 1
```

Then addition and subtraction...

```
answer = 11
```

If required, you can change the order of operations by placing brackets round the ones to be performed first.

Here we go again:

```
answer = 2^(2+ 4) * 6 / (3 - 1)
```

First the bracketed operations...

```
answer = 2^6 * 6 / 2
```

Then ^ exponentiation...

```
answer = 64 * 6 / 2
```

Next multiplication and division...

```
answer = 192
```

Practical examples

Test the arithmetic operators by creating this program. It allows you to input any two numbers then find the result of the arithmetic operations. First set up the form:

1 Place on a form three TextBoxes, named *Number1*, *Number2* and *Result*.

2 Next place six Buttons, labelling and naming them to suit the operators + − * / \ and Mod.

3 Place an exit Button to give the program a tidy end.

4 The code on all the Buttons is almost the same. Here's what you need on the Plus Button:

```
Result.Text = Val(Number1.Text) + Val(Number2.Text)
```

5 For the other Buttons, simply change the operator.

The Val() function is only essential for the + operator as this can also work with text ("A" + "B" = "AB"). It ensures that the contents of the TextBoxes are treated as number values. Miss it out and you will find that 2 + 2 = 22.

1.15 Assignment operators

To assign a value to a variable we use the '=' sign, e.g.

```
topLimit = 1000
count = count + 1
```

If the same variable appears on both sides of the expression – i.e. if you are performing a calculation on a variable and storing the result in it – you can use the assignment operators. These combine the '=' sign with the arithmetic operators:

```
+=      -=      *=      /=      \=      ^=
```

A simple example would be for handling a running total:

```
Total += Item
```

This is the same as:

```
Total = Total + Item
```

If you have long variable names, you will appreciate the reduction in the amount of typing:

```
UsersCurrentBankBalance -= LatestWithdrawal
```

Joining text

We have already noted that you can join text strings together with "+". The "&" (ampersand) does exactly the same job, and has the advantage of making it very clear in the code that you are joining text not adding numbers. This is more important when you are working with variables, instead of literal text or number values.

```
firstName = "Roger"

surname = "Dodger"

fullName = firstName & " " & surname        'why the space?
```

This results in fullName holding "Rodger Dodger".

There is also a '&=' assignment operator, which will add text onto the end of the current string:

```
Output.Text &= NextWord
```

1.16 Exercises

1.1   Set up a form containing a TextBox, a Label and a Button. The Text on the Label should ask the user to enter a name. Edit the TextBox's Text property to leave it blank. Attach code to the Button so that when it is clicked, the Label displays the user's name.

1.2   Add a Button that will end the program when clicked. The only code needed in the Click procedure is the single word End.

1.3   Edit the various Font properties of the Label, to give large, bright text on a striking background.

1.4   Set up a new form containing one Label and three Buttons. Edit the Buttons' Text to read "Stop", "Go" and "End". Attach code to these Buttons so that the first makes the Label display "Stop", the second makes it display "Go", and the third ends the program.

2 Designing and creating programs

The best way to learn a program language is to write programs in it! So, let's get on with it. In this chapter we'll work through the stages – program design, interface construction, coding and building/testing – to produce a program.

2.1 Program design

The traditional methods of program design, such as JSP, flowcharts, top-down design, work well for traditional programming languages. With these, the program forms a continuous whole with a distinct structure and sequence of activities. The sequence may branch or loop, but there is always something happening – even if it is only waiting for an input. With an event-driven, object-oriented language like Visual Basic, a different approach is needed.

In Visual Basic, most operations are executed in response to an event linked to an object, and at any one point there could be a number of events which could occur. The operation may be set to run its full course, or be left open to interruption by other events. The event may be, for example, a keyboard input, the movement or click of a mouse, a timer reaching its critical point or the loading of a form. When the operation is complete, the program reverts to *idle-time* – waiting for something to happen. You don't have to write code to cover this, for it is handled by the Visual Basic system. There are low-level routines already in place to scan the keyboard, the mouse, the timers and other sources of events. You do not have to write code to trap the events. Your job is to specify what happens next. While most events will be activated by the user, they can also be triggered from within the program itself. The design method must be capable of handling this interplay of objects, events and operations. Let's see how it works in practice.

2.2 The Launch program

This first program, designed to launch you into Visual Basic, shows several different examples of this interplay. I hope that it also shows how little code is needed to create good effects – in this case, a rocket launch.

The launch is produced by changing the **Top** property (which determines the vertical position) of a control to make it move up the screen. Other effects are also produced by changing properties during the execution of the program. Some of these have a fundamental impact. Notice the way that **Enabled** can be set to *False*, so that a control will no longer respond to events, and **Visible** set to *False,* to make a control disappear.

Before you start, take a few minutes to go into Paint and draw yourself a rocket! Make it fairly small – around 200 pixels high.

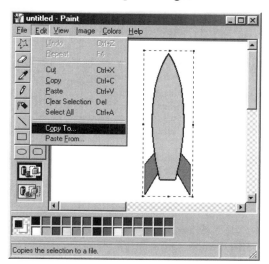

Figure 2.1

Creating an image in Paint. The **Edit > Copy To** command allows you to save a selected part of the canvas as a file.

2.3 The user interface

This is not just a fancy term for the screen display, though that is part of the interface. It also covers how the program interacts with the user. How does the user input data, and what information is returned to the user? In designing the form, we have to think in terms of what controls are needed and how they should be arranged for best effect. With the launch program, we want the user to be able to set the flight speed, to launch the rocket, to start again and to exit from the program.

Launch, reset and exit are all simple jobs that can be handled neatly by Buttons. The launch cannot take place until the speed has been set, so that Button must be turned off at first. The *Enabled* property will let us do this. Setting the speed could be done in a number of ways, of which the simplest is probably to type it into a TextBox. If its Text property is set to "Enter speed" at the start, then this will give the necessary prompt to the user. A little label by the speed TextBox would be useful. Lastly, of course, we must have a PictureBox to handle the rocket image.

Having decided what controls are needed, we can plan their layout. This is best done on paper first, as part of the overall planning process. While you are thinking out where things will go, you should also be thinking about how they will interact, and jotting down notes on the plan. (See Figure 2.2.) The design for the code should then grow naturally out of the form design.

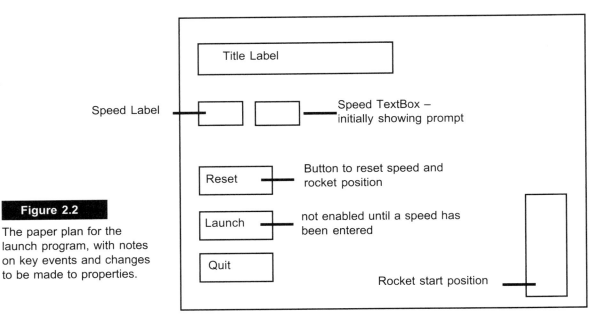

Figure 2.2

The paper plan for the launch program, with notes on key events and changes to be made to properties.

2.4 Code design

The code here is almost entirely concerned with changing properties. The lines for this all take the shape:

```
control.property = newvalue
```

(Note the full stop between the control name and the property. Whatever you give as the *newvalue* must be enclosed in quotes if it is text.)

As long as you know the name of the control, the property that you want to change and the new value, these lines present no problems. You can explore the changes by testing them in the Properties window, while you are working on the Form design.

We can plan the code with a simple top-down design. With the three Buttons, the code will be activated by the `Click` event.

Reset button

```
reset the Rocket's Top to place it near the bottom of the Form

turn off the Launch button's Enabled

change the Speed TextBox's Text to "Enter speed"

place the cursor in the text box, ready for the user
```

That last action will be achieved by the line:

```
txtSpeed.Focus()
```

The `Focus()` method prepares a control for keyboard input. (And note the empty brackets at the end of its name – if you miss these out, the Studio's syntax checker will add them for you.) Used on a TextBox, Focus() places the cursor there; used on a Button, it highlights it and sets it so that pressing **[Enter]** acts the same as a mouse click. It is not essential here, for the users can put the cursor in the text box themselves, but it makes life easier for them.

Launch button

```
start to loop
    subtract the speed from the the Rocket's Top to lift it
    wait a moment - the PC's far too fast
    check for other events
loop back until the Rocket is off the screen
```

Here we can use a `Do  Loop` to keep the rocket moving. The basic structure is:

```
Do

    . . .

Loop Until test
```

This will make the program cycle round the enclosed lines until the test proves true, and in this case the test will check the Rocket's **Top** property. (See Chapter 3 for more on this structure.)

A modern PC processes information so quickly that you have to find some means of slowing things down if you want to see movement on screen. The solution here has been to write a delay loop – it gets the PC to count up to 1,000,000. There are better ways of producing timed activity which we will look at later.

Unless we do something about it, the execution will lock into the loop until it reaches its end. As we want our users to be able to change the speed or restart the launch while the rocket is in flight, we must make the system check for these events, within the loop. The solution is provided by the `DoEvents()` method. Its full name is `Application.DoEvents()` as it belongs to the Application class – i.e., the whole program – rather than to a control within it. The method returns control to the system, to check if an event has occurred, and if it has, the system will respond to that event before going back into the loop.

Quit button

```
end the program
```

All we need here is the `End` statement that we met earlier.

Speed text box

```
enable the Launch button when something is typed in
```

Among the events handled by TextBoxes are `Keypress` and `TextChanged`, both of which are triggered by the user typing in data. Keypress raises issues that are best left until later. `TextChanged` can cope with all we want here. It will pick up any activity in the TextBox, and we can assume that the user is typing in a valid value. (If we were trying to make this program idiot-proof, we would assume nothing.)

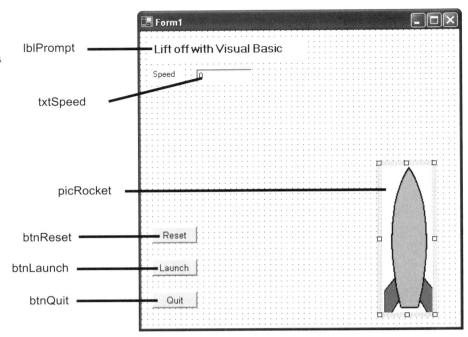

Figure 2.3

The launch Form,
showing the controls
and their Names

lblPrompt

txtSpeed

picRocket

btnReset

btnLaunch

btnQuit

2.5   The form and the controls

The first job is to lay out the controls on the form. In this case, they can go anywhere that pleases you, as long as you keep a clear flightpath for the rocket. The next job is to set their initial properties – including their Names.

Naming controls

If a control is going to be used actively by the program, it should be given a meaningful name to replace the default *Label1*, *TextBox2* or whatever. The name should be a reminder of the nature of the control and its purpose in the program. A common convention in Visual Basic is to start names with a prefix to indicate the control, followed by one or more words, all run together but each starting with capitals, e.g. *btnQuit*.

In this program we have Buttons (*btn*), a TextBox (*txt*), a Label (*lbl*) and a PictureBox (*pic*). The names are shown in Figure 2.3.

Setting properties

Type the Text for the Buttons and Label, setting the fonts and colours as you like.

Set the *btnLaunch*.**Enabled** property to *False*. When the program starts, its Text will be displayed in grey, rather than black, and the Button will not respond to a click. It will be enabled again by the Change event on *txtSpeed*.

To get the picture into *picRocket*, select the **Image** property of the control and click the ... Button to open this dialog box:

Figure 2.4

Loading a file into a
Picture control

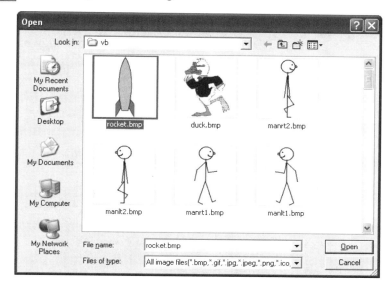

Work your way through the folders to get to the right place, then select the graphic from the files. Click **Open** to load the file into the control and to exit from the dialog box.

2.6 Writing the code

To attach code to an object's event, double-click on the object to open the Code window. The system will generate the header and end lines for the sub to handle the object's most commonly used event – such as Click for a Button. You switch to another event, but in this program that will be not be necessary.

Note these points before you start to type in the code:

- You can ignore the lines starting with a quote. These are **comment lines** to help explain the code. In this book comments are shown in bold to make them stand out – on screen they are usually in green. Comments can be written at the end of active lines, or on lines by themselves – the system ignores any text after a single quote.

- Do not include the first or last lines of the subs – they will be in place already.

- When you are defining an object's property, after typing the dot at the end of the name, a list of properties and methods belonging to the object will appear. Type the first letters of the property, or use the arrow keys to select it, then press **[Tab]** to write it into your code.

- Press **[Enter]** or the Down arrow key at the end of each line. The system will then check your typing and alert you to any errors. Some errors will not be spotted, e.g. if you mistype the name of a control, Visual Basic may assume that you mean another control or a variable.

Start with *btnReset*, and type in the lines shown below.

```
Private Sub btnReset_Click(ByVal sender As System.Object, ByVal e As
System.EventArgs) Handles btnReset.Click
  picRocket.Top = 200
  txtSpeed.Text = "Enter speed"
  ' turn off the Launch button
  btnLaunch.Enabled = False
  ' place the cursor in the Speed TextBox
  txtSpeed.Focus()
End Sub
```

When the *btnReset_Click* code is done, click back onto the Form and double-click the next control to which you want to add code.

```
Private Sub btnLaunch_Click(ByVal sender As System.Object, ByVal e As
System.EventArgs) Handles btnLaunch.Click
  'Timer1.Enabled = True
  Dim delay As Long          ' Long variables can take huge numbers
  Do
     picRocket.Top = picRocket.Top - Val(txtSpeed.Text)
     For delay = 1 To 1000000        ' Try different values here
     Next
     Application.DoEvents()
  Loop Until picRocket.Top < -250      ' Set a limit to suit
End Sub
```

Note the line that changes the Rocket's **Top** value.

```
     picRocket.Top = picRocket.Top - Val(txtSpeed.Text)
```

We want to subtract from it the number held in the **Text** property of the *txtSpeed* box. The `Val()` function converts this to a number value. This is not essential, as Visual Basic will automatically convert text to numbers in this kind of situation.

```
Private Sub txtSpeed_TextChanged(ByVal sender As System.Object, ByVal
e As System.EventArgs) Handles txtSpeed.TextChanged
  btnLaunch.Enabled = True ' turn on the Launch button
End Sub
```

Don't worry about the header lines

There's a lot in those header lines of subs, most of which can be ignored at this stage. The brackets specify what kind of information is passed into and out of the sub, and what it is called. We will be looking at this later on, but for the moment leave them as they are generated by the system and concentrate on the code that goes into the body of the sub.

```
    Private Sub btnQuit_Click(ByVal sender As System.Object, ByVal e As
System.EventArgs) Handles btnQuit.Click
    End
End Sub
```

2.7   Running and testing

Set the program in motion with the **Debug > Start** command, or by pressing **[F5]**. The system will check your code again, and this time it will look at the interaction between the different lines. If any errors are noted, it will open the code window at the relevant place, with the error highlighted.

Play with the program. Set the speed and launch the rocket. Use the **Reset** Button to reset the rocket on its pad. Try changing the speed, or restarting, while the rocket is in motion. Test every possible sequence of events.

While you are doing this, think about what is happening beneath the surface, about the interplay between the objects as events are handled. Take any point in the program and note what events are waiting to happen.

For instance, after **Reset** has been pressed, there are three events which could be triggered:

`btnReset_Click` would get you back to where you were;

`txtSpeed_TextChanged` would enable the Launch Button, and set the speed;

`cmdQuit_Click` would end the program.

Task 2.1

Quit the program. Back at the Design window, double-click the Launch Button to get into its code. Type a single quote at the start of the **DoEvents** line. When you move the cursor off this line, the text will change colour to show that this is now a comment – not an active part of the code. Run the program again and try to restart, or change the speed, while the rocket is in motion. You should find that it is impossible. Without **DoEvents**, the system cannot trap events when it is executing code.

2.8   Printouts

When developing programs, it can sometimes be useful to have a full printout of the code – trying to follow what you are doing to a variable or object in different parts of a program can be hard if you have to jump backwards and forwards through the code on screen. It is much simpler when you can read the code from sheets laid out in front of you.

To get a printout of the program code, go into the Code window and use the menu command **File > Print**. If it is a long program, and you only need to see part of it, set the print range in the dialog box.

If required, you can include the details of the controls and their properties in your printout. Click the ⊞ icon by the side of "Windows Form Designer Generated Code" to open up the lines generated by the system when you placed and defined the controls.

If you need a picture of the layout of the form, go to the Design window, adjust it if necessary to display the form fully then press **[Alt]** + **[PrintScreen]**. This will put a copy of the screen display in the Clipboard. Paste it into Paint or any graphics software, and print from there.

2.9   Exercises

2.1   Using the techniques illustrated in the Launch program, design and build a program that will move a picture across the screen. For a more impressive display, create a background picture and drop this into the BackgroundImage property of the Form.

2.2   The aim here is to produce an annotated diagram. Set up a Form with a large PictureBox above and a large Label below. Draw or scan a picture of a computer, save the file and load it into the PictureBox's Image. Place small Buttons beside key components on the PictureBox, with the Texts set to match the components. Attach code to each of these Buttons so that, when clicked, they display information about the component in the Label.

2.3   Write a program to convert temperatures from Celsius to Fahrenheit, using the formula:

```
DegreesF = DegreesC * 9 / 5 + 32
```

Hint: Use TextBoxes to take the input in Celsius and display the result in Fahrenheit. The conversion code can be attached to the TextChanged event of the Celsius TextBox, or to the Click event of a Button (captioned "Convert"). Include a "Quit" Button on the Form, to end the program properly.

2.4   Adapt the program developed in 2.3 so that it can convert temperatures from either form to the other. To change Fahrenheit to Celsius use the formula:

```
DegreesC = (DegreesF - 32) * 5 / 9
```

Hint: If you try to run the conversion routines from the TextChanged events of both TextBoxes, you will hit a snag. As each TextChanged routine would alter the value in the other TextBox, it would trigger its TextChanged event and alter the value in the box that was being typed in – chaos! Use suitably captioned Buttons instead.

3 Program flow

The overall flow of a program is largely controlled by the user's interaction with the screen objects, as we noted in the last chapter and to which we shall return again, but if anything interesting is to happen when an object is selected, we must control the flow of execution within routines.

3.1 Controlling the flow

Program flow can be considered under two main headings – *branches* and *loops*.

With a branch, the execution will flow down one of two or more paths, depending upon the result of a logical test. The relevant structures here are `If ... Then ... Else` (and variants), and `Select Case`. The `GoTo` jump may be used in conjunction with `If` to skip over a set of lines. `GoTo` is reviled by purists as its use can lead to horribly tangled code, but there are times when it offers a convenient solution.

With loops – the iteration of a block of code – the number of repetitions may be controlled by a logical test, using one of the many variations of the `Do ... Loop`. Where the loop is to run a fixed number of times, the `For ... Next` structure offers the simplest solution.

3.2 Logical testing

Logical tests may be performed upon string or numeric *expressions*, or upon controls. (The latter raises complications that we will not dwell on here.) The expressions may contain variables, literal values, functions and arithmetic or other operators, as long as the expressions produce suitable values. Examples of expressions:

Surname, X, Y	Variables, used alone
"LETMEIN", 99, 0	Literal values
X * 2	Calculations including variables and values
LEN(Surname), CHR(Num)	Functions producing numeric or string values.

A test will result in either a *True*, *False* or *Null* value. *Null* occurs when one or more of the expressions being tested has a null value, i.e. it involves a variable that does not hold any value. For most purposes, *Null* and *False* can be taken as the same.

Logical tests normally use the comparison operators, e.g. `If X > 1000` but you can test on an expression directly. The expression `If X Then...` is *True* if *X* holds a non-zero value.

Comparison operators

Visual Basic can use these operators to compare values:

=	Equal to	<>	Greater or Less than (not Equal to)
<	Less than	>	Greater than
<=	Less than or Equals to	>=	Greater than or Equal to
Like	'Fuzzy' string comparisons	**Is**	Compares control variables

Functions and arithmetic operators have a higher priority than comparison operators, which means that expressions are evaluated before the test.

Test	Result	Why?
99 <= 10 * 5	False	10 * 5 = 50
LEN("Fred") < 10	True	"Fred" has 4 characters

When used with string expressions, the operators can compare the characters in two ways based on the **Option Compare** settings. The default setting is **Binary**, which compares ASCII values. This can lead to apparently unusual results.

Test	Result	Why?
"A" < "B"	True	ASCII "A" = 65 and ASCII "B" = 66
"a" < "B"	False	ASCII "a" = 97
"Bee" < "Beekeeper"	True	They are equal up to "Bee", but the second goes on, and any character is greater than nothing.
"Anteater" > "ant"	False	ASCII "A" = 65, ASCII "a" = 97

Option Compare can also be set to Text, which runs simple alphabetic comparisons, where "A" = "a". To set the option, write it in at the very top of the code:

```
Option Compare Text
Public Class Form1
```

Where numbers are taken from TextBoxes, they may be treated as strings. When in doubt, use **Val()** to force the conversion from string to number.

Test	Result	Why?
"99" < "100"	False	The test compares text, not number, values and ASCII "9" = 57, ASCII "1" = 49.
Val("99")<Val("100")	True	The Val() functions yield number values

Like

This allows you to make inexact matches, finding strings that only have some characters in common. The comparisons are made using *wildcards* – special characters that can stand for any other single character or set. The wildcards are:

? Any single character

\# Any single digit

* Zero or more characters

[set] Any character in the set defined by its first and last character

[!set]   Any character *except* those in the defined set

Some examples may help.

Surname Like "Sm?th"	True for "Smith" and "Smyth"
Fname Like "*.DTA"	True for any file with ".DTA" extension
Digit Like "[0-9]"	True for any digit, but no other characters
LowLetter Like "[a-z]"	True for any single lowercase letter
PicNum Like "Fig[0-9]"	True for "Fig0", "Fig1", "Fig2", etc.
NonDigit Like "[!0-9]"	True for anything except the digits

Note that there are quotes around the whole expression.

Is can only be used with control variables and raises points that are too complex to deal with at this level.

Logical operators

The logical operators are mainly used to combine two or more relational operations in a test. There are six:

Not	Used with a single expression, to reverse its value, so that True becomes False and vice versa.
And	Links two expressions and is True if both expressions are True.
Or	*True* if either or both expressions are True.
Xor	(Exclusive OR) True if one or other – but not both – expressions are True.
AndAlso	A more efficient version of **And**, this stops checking if it finds that the first expression is False.
OrElse	A more efficient version of **Or**, this stops checking if the first test proves True.

Brackets in logical expressions

Where a test uses two or more logical operators, they are evaluated in the same order in which they are listed above. If you want to change the priority – perhaps to evaluate an OR before an AND – enclose the OR part in brackets. Examples of logical operations:

```
... X > 1000 AND Y > 1000...
```

True if both X and Y are over their limits

```
...X > 1000 XOR Y > 1000...
```

True if either of them are over their limits, but False if they both are over (or below).

```
...NOT ( X > 1000 EQU Y > 1000)
```

This gives exactly the same results as the previous test – work it out and see.

```
...X > 100 AND Y > 100 OR X < 0...
```

True if either X and Y are both over their limits, or X is negative – in which case the Y is irrelevant.

```
...Y > 100 AND ( X > 100 OR X < 0)...
```

True if Y is over 100 and X is above or below its limits.

3.3   Branching with If

Though based on the `If...Then...Else...` test found in most languages, Visual Basic's version has several variations and traps for the unwary. In all cases, `If` is followed by a logical test and the keyword `Then`. What happens next varies.

Single line branching

Where only a small amount of code is dependent upon the test, the whole structure can be conveniently written on a single line, following one or other of these patterns.

```
If test Then statement(s)-if-true
If test Then statement(s)-if-true Else statement(s)-if-false
```

Examples:

```
If age < 16 Then status = "Junior"
If password = "itsme" Then Msgbox("Hi") Else Msgbox("Bye"):End
```

In the first example, nothing happens if the *age* value is 16 or more. In the second, the presence of the `Else` clause means that action is taken if a wrong password is given. The action here consists of two statements, one producing a message, the other ending the program. Note that where there are several statements, they are separated by colons (:).

Multi-line Ifs

There is no theoretical limit to the number of statements you can include in a single line `If` structure, for the whole line can be as long as you like. In practice, long lines are awkward to view on screen and likely to be a source of error, simply because you cannot see clearly what they are doing.

If more than one statement is dependent upon the truth or falsity of the test, it is best to split the structure over several lines.

```
If test Then
   statement-if-true-1
   statement-if-true-2
   . . .
Else : statement-if-false-1
   statement-if-false-2
   . . .
End If
```

Note the `End If` at the end of the structure. This is not needed with a single line `If`, but essential with the multi-line variant. If you write a statement on the same line as `Else`, you need a colon as punctuation (and if you miss it out, the syntax checker will write it in for you). It is probably simpler, and more readable, to push the statement after Else down to the next line.

A simple multi-line `If` might look like this:

```
If age < 16 Then
   Status = "Junior"
   ClubFees = 7.5
Else
   Status = "Senior"
   ClubFees = 25
End If
```

In this case, status and club fees are dependent upon the age of the member, with only two alternatives, based on the 16 limit. Where there are several alternative routes to the flow, the structure can be extended by an `ElseIf` clause – or by more than one – each followed by its own logical test and a `Then`.

Try this example. Write it into the `Click` procedure of a Button, run the program, click on the Button and type in a value.

ElseIf ... Example

```
Private Sub Button1_Click (ByVal sender As System.Object, ByVal e
As System.EventArgs) Handles Button1.Click
Dim salary As Single

salary = InputBox("How much do you want to earn?")
If salary > 50000 Then
   MsgBox "Don't go into writing"
ElseIf salary > 20000 Then
   MsgBox "Good luck"
Else
   MsgBox "What modest aims!"
End If
End Sub
```

This form of the structure is appropriate where you want to test a value against several limits, or where you have second and subsequent tests that are only to be performed if the first one proves false.

Nested Ifs

The statement that follows `Then` or `Else` can be another `If` structure. This can be a single line or a multi-line one – in which case it must be closed by its own `End If`. These can get complicated. It is all too easy to lose track of which `End If` relates to which `If`. Good layout will help to keep things clearer. You may have noticed that I have indented the statements in the examples above, so that the structure stands out. Where one `If` structure is nested within another, its keywords should be indented, keeping the `If`, `Else` and `End If` in line, and their statements indented further.

If layout is important for displaying the structure after you have written it, design is crucial for getting it right in the first place. Start by drawing up a JSP diagram, or decision tree, so that you are clear about the logic and the nature of each branch.

For example, suppose you wanted a routine that would work out the correct form of address, based on the user's age and sex. (We will ignore marital status and address all adult females as 'Ms'.)

Figure 3.1

JSP diagram for a routine to decide the form-of-address

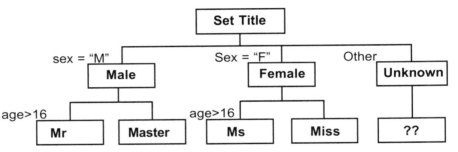

Task 3.1

Write a routine to implement this design, using nested Ifs. Type it into a Form_Click procedure and test out each branch. A possible solution is given at the end of the chapter.

3.4 Select Case

Where you have many alternative routes all based on the values that may be held in one variable, the `Select Case` structure provides a clearer solution than a set of `If`s or one long multi-branched `If`. The basic shape is:

```
Select Case variable
   Case values_1
      actions if variable = values_1
      further actions if variable = values_1
   Case value_2
      actions if variable = values_2
```

```
        ...
     Case Else
        actions if variable = any other value
     End Select
```

The layout is important. Each `Case` must be on a new line, and the actions that follow from a `Case` must start on a line below – they cannot be run along the same line.

```
     Case Value_1   actions ...
```

This will produce an error report.

Any string or numeric variable can be used in a `Select Case`. The values that follow each `Case` can be a single item, a range joined by the keyword `To`, or a set of alternatives linked by commas.

`Case Else` is optional, but a good way to handle unexpected values. Note that the structure must be closed by `End Select`.

This fragment of code is taken from the maths test program, given in full in section 4.12. It shows the structure at its simplest. The values in the variable *sumtype* can only be "+", "-", "*" or "/" and each initiates a single action.

```
     Select Case sumtype
        Case "+"
           z = x + y
        Case "-"
           z = x - y
        Case "*"
           z = x * y
        Case "/"
           z = x / y
        End Select
```

Worked example

A more complex `Select Case` structure is shown below. This handles single values, ranges and sets. It takes in a character through an InputBox, and delivers a different message depending upon the nature of the character.

```
Private Sub Button1_Click (ByVal sender As System.Object, ByVal e
As System.EventArgs) Handles Button1.Click
Dim c As Char
char = InputBox("Enter a character")
Select Case c
   Case "!"                              ' single value
      MsgBox ("Shriek", 48)
      End                                ' ends the program
   Case "0" To "9"                       ' range "0" to  "9" inclusive
      MsgBox ("Digit")
   Case "A" To "Z", "a" To "z"
   ' two ranges, capitals and lower case
      MsgBox ("Letter")
   Case "(", ")", "{", "}", "[", "]"     ' set of alternatives
      MsgBox ("Bracket")
```

```
     Case Else                        ' for everything else
        MsgBox ("Symbol ASCII Code " & Asc(c))
   End Select
   End Sub
```

> ## Task 3.2
>
> Copy the code into a Button's Click sub. Test it with a range of values that will activate each *Case*. What happens if you enter a word instead of a single character?

3.5 GoTo

I think this is only included because there are some old dyed-in-the-wool Basic programmers who could not contemplate life without it. The fact is that GoTo tends to produce tangled code and is only needed in Resume statements in error trapping (see Chapter 5). Anything that you can do with a GoTo, you can do more easily in another way. If you want to repeat lines, use a For ... Next or a Loop. If you want to bypass a block of code, it is neater and simpler to make the block into a sub (see section 3.8).

But if you really must use GoTo, here's how.

The jump can be forwards or backwards, but must be in the same procedure. Mark the target point in the code with a label. This can be a number or a word, written with a following colon. It can be on a separate line above, or at the start of the line containing the first statement in the target block.

The GoTo can be written as a single line statement or incorporated in an If ... Then. It is followed by the label name – without the colon. For example, here are two GoTos – one used to repeat a set of lines, the other to jump out of the loop when the target value is reached. Compare this tangled code with the more elegant Loops shown below.

```
Private Sub Button1_Click (ByVal sender As System.Object, ByVal e
As System.EventArgs) Handles Button1.Click
Dim x As Integer
x = 0
startloop:
   x = x + 1
   MsgBox(x)
   If x = 10 Then GoTo endloop
   GoTo startloop
endloop:
MsgBox ("Done")
End
End Sub
```

3.6 For ... Next

Visual Basic's `For ... Next` structure is almost the same as that of traditional Basics, and more flexible than Pascal's. In this formal definition, optional features are enclosed in [brackets]. You will note that much is optional:

```
For variable = start_value To end_value [Step size]
   statements...
   [Exit For]
   statements...
Next [variable]
```

Start_value and *end_value* can be any numbers, variables or expressions that produce suitable values. They do not have to be integer. If the `Step` *size* is omitted, the loop counter will be increased by one each time, otherwise the `Step` can be any whole or fractional value, either positive or negative. The variable name after the `Next` is not essential, but does make the code easier to read.

`Exit For` provides an escape route, should you need to break out of the loop before the end value has been reached. As you would normally use `For ... Next` loops to run through a fixed range of values, this feature will rarely be wanted.

`For ... Next` loops can be nested within one another. Indenting your code, and writing the variable names in the `Next` lines will help to ensure that inner loops are indeed completed within the outer ones.

A `For ... Next` loop can be as simple as this:

```
For num = 1 To 10
   MsgBox(num)
Next
```

Or it may use all the 'optional extras', as in this next example.

```
Private Sub Button1_Click(ByVal sender As System.Object, ByVal e As
System.EventArgs) Handles Button1.Click
   Dim num, x, star As Integer
   Output.Text = ""
   For num = 1 To 20 Step 2
      x = Int(Rnd() * 30) + 1
      For star = 1 To x
         Output.Text &= "*"
         If star > 20 Then Exit For
      Next star
      Output.Text &= Chr(13) & Chr(10)   ' start a new line
   Next num
End Sub
```

Task 3.3

Add a RichTextBox (deep enough for at least 10 lines of text) and a Button to a form. Name the RichTextBox *Output*. Copy the code into a Button's Click sub. Run the program and click on the Button to find out what it does. How could you simplify the `For num` line and still get the same results?

3.7   Do loops

These offer the most flexible way to repeat a set of lines. We used the `Do ... Loop` **Until** version in the last chapter, but the structure has a number of variations. They can be summarised in these formats:

1   Do Until or **While** test
```
        statements ...
        ... [Exit Do]
    Loop
```

2   Do
```
        statements ...
        ... [Exit Do]
    Loop Until or While test
```

Some things remain the same – there is always a `Do` at the start and `Loop` at the end, and there must be an exit test somewhere, or the loop will run until it crashes the system.

If the exit test is written in the `Do` line, the loop will not be executed if the test is satisfied; if it is written into the `Loop` line, the loop will be executed at least once.

In either position, the test may use either the `Until` or `While` keyword. The two are effectively the same, except that the logic of a `While` test is reversed. `While test is true` is the same as `Until test is not true`. Use whichever gives the clearest test.

As a final option, you can omit the test from either start or end and rely on an `Exit Do` to break out of the loop. This would normally be activated with an `If` test. The following loops all produce exactly the same results. Notice how the comparison operators and test values vary to suit the `Until` or `While` expressions.

Test at the start
```
num = 1                       or        num = 1
Do Until num = 11                       Do While num <= 10
   Print num                               Print num
   num = num + 1                           num = num + 1
Loop                                    Loop
```

Test at the end
```
num = 1                       or        num = 1
Do                                      Do
   Print num                               Print num
   num = num + 1                           num = num + 1
Loop Until num = 11                     Loop While num <= 10
```

Test in the middle
```
num = 1
Do
   Print num
   If num = 10 Then Exit Do
   num = num + 1
Loop
```

3.8 Subroutines and functions

Subroutines and functions, both off-the-peg and tailor-made, are central to Visual Basic. So far, all the subs and functions that we have used have been those built into the system, or those written to handle events from controls, and you can get a long way with those alone. However, there are times when you can produce a more readable and efficient program by writing subs and functions of your own. Readability is improved because it is easier to make sense of small blocks of code that do specific jobs, than of long routines that perform a variety of operations. Efficiency is improved when you need to perform the same operation at several different places in the program. Writing a common piece of code into a sub, and calling it from each point, can save a lot of time and effort.

Subs

A sub is a block of code that performs some kind of operation. Up until now you have probably only used subs that are linked to events. A free-standing sub is used like a method, such as `MsgBox()`. It is executed when it is *called* from somewhere else in the program, and at the end of its run, the flow will pass back to the point from which it was called. Values may be passed to the procedure through *parameters* (also known as *arguments*), and the sub may pass changed values back to the code that called it, or leave them unchanged.

The essential nature of the sub is defined in its first line. This takes the form:

```
AccessType Sub name (ByVal/ByRef arg_1 As Type, ByVal/
ByRef arg_2 As Type,...)
```

The *AccessType* determines the scope of the sub. The key ones to note are `Private` which specifies that the sub can only be accessed from within the same form or module, and `Public` which allows it to be accessed from anywhere in the program.

The parameters are optional, though the brackets must be there, even if empty. `ByVal` or `ByRef` affects what happens to any variables that are passed to the procedure by the calling code. If `ByVal` is used, only the value of the variable is passed to the sub, and its original value is unchanged in the calling code. `ByRef` passes the variable itself to the sub, so changes made there are retained on return to the program.

The end of a procedure is marked by `End Sub`. If necessary, an early exit from the procedure can be forced by the `Exit Sub` statement.

Functions

A function is a block of code that returns a value to calling code. They will almost always take parameters, as the main purpose of functions is to convert values from one form to another. They appear in the calling code as values being assigned to variables, or used in expressions, or displayed on screen.

The syntax of function definitions is almost identical to that of a procedure:

```
AccessType Function name ( arguments ) As Type
```

At some point in the function, there must be a line that copies the calculated value to the function name, for passing back to the calling code. It takes the shape:

```
name = value
```

3.9   Creating a sub

The simplest kind of sub has no parameters. You would use one where you wanted to be able to run the same block of code from two or more places, e.g. where the same operation can be started from a menu option or a toolbar tool (see Chapter 4).

Here's a trivial example. To make this work, you will need a Label (called *Label1*) as the sub changes the text displayed there, switching between "Hello" and "Goodbye". You will also need a Button – it is from here that you will call the sub.

Go into the code window, and type this code at any convenient point – before or after any existing sub.

```
Private Sub ChangeMessage()
    If Label1.Text = "Hello" Then
       Label1.Text = "Goodbye"
    Else
       Label1.Text = "Hello"
    End If
End Sub
```

To see it in action, write a calling line into the Click event of the Button.

```
Private Sub Button1_Click(ByVal sender As System.Object,
ByVal e As System.EventArgs) Handles Button1.Click
    ChangeMessage()
End Sub
```

Now let's try it with parameters. This sub takes in a string of text and displays it in the same Label.

```
Private Sub NewMessage(ByVal message As String)
    Label1.Text = message
End Sub
```

It is called by lines like this:

```
NewMessage("Calling you from the main program")
```

or

```
Dim myText As String = "Calling all subs!"
NewMessage(myText)
```

The next thing to explore is the difference between ByVal and ByRef. Try this.

Create the following sub. It accepts into *n*, the variable declared as a parameter, whatever integer value is passed from the calling code. It displays the contents of *n*, then assigns a new value to it.

```
Private Sub display(ByVal n As Integer)
    MsgBox("The number passed to the sub is " & n)
    n = 0
End Sub
```

Rewrite the code in the Button Click event so that it creates an integer variable, assigns a value to it and passes that to the display() sub. It ends by displaying the current value in the variable.

```
Private Sub Button1_Click(ByVal sender As System.Object,
ByVal e As System.EventArgs) Handles Button1.Click
    Dim num1 As Integer
    num1 = 99
    display(num1)
    MsgBox("After calling Num1 holds " & num1)
End Sub
```

When you run the program you should see that the value of 99 has been passed to display() and that the variable still holds this value on return. Whatever is done to *n* – the parameter that links to *Num1* – the changes remain within the sub.

Now change the first line of display() so that the variable is passed ByRef, and build and run the program again.

```
Private Sub display(ByRef n As Integer)
```

This time you should see that the value in *Num1* has been changed to 0.

With ByVal, the value only is passed to the sub, so that the variable in the calling code is untouched.

With ByRef, the address of the variable in the calling code is passed to the sub. Changing the value of the parameter means changing the value stored at that address – which is the calling code's variable's address.

3.10   Creating a function

The process here is much the same as with a sub, except that we must define the type of the returned value, and include a line that will return it. Try this example – especially if you dislike radians. It converts radians to degrees using the formula:

```
AngleInDegrees = AngleInRadians * 360 / 2 * Pi
```

This works because 360 degrees = 2 * Pi radians. If you prefer, the end part can be simplified to 180 / Pi.

```
Function degrees (ByVal rads As Double) As Double
    Dim Pi As Double
    Pi = 4 * Atn(1)
    degrees = rads * 180 / Pi        'pass the result out
End Function
```

The line beginning with the function name '**degrees** = ' is crucial. This is the one that gets the result out of the function.

Write a suitable test routine that includes a line like this:

```
AngleInDegs = degrees(CDbl(AngleInRads))
```

Note that when calling functions, the arguments are enclosed in brackets.

(The CDbl() function will not be needed if *AngleInRads* is defined as a Double.)

> ### Task 3.4
>
> Write a function that will convert angles in degrees into radians. The formula is the reverse of the earlier one:
> ```
> AngleInRadians = AngleInDegrees * Pi / 180
> ```

3.11 Recursive functions

A recursive function is one which calls itself. This can be the most effective way to handle some kinds of mathematical operations. The two key points to remember when writing recursive functions are:

- somewhere there must be a line with the function name on both the left and the right sides of an = sign, which is where the function calls itself;
- somewhere else there must be a statement that passes a definite value to the function. This is the escape route. Without it, the function would call itself endlessly, until it crashed the system.

Factorials provide a clear, simple demonstration. A factorial is a number multiplied by every other whole number below it, down to 1, e.g.

$$\text{Factorial } 3 = 3 \times 2 \times 1$$
$$\text{Factorial } 4 = 4 \times 3 \times 2 \times 1$$
$$\text{Factorial } 5 = 5 \times 4 \times 3 \times 2 \times 1$$

Think about it, and you will see that Factorial 5 could be found by $5 \times$ Factorial 4; Factorial 4 by $4 \times$ Factorial 3, and so on.

From this, we can derive the general rule:

```
Factorial n = n * Factorial (n-1)
```

As Factorial (1–1) is 0, the rule is different for 1:

```
Factorial 1 = 1
```

From these two rules we can define the function.

```
Function Factorial (num As Double) As Double
   If num = 1 Then
      Factorial = 1                        ' the escape route
   Else
      Factorial = num * Factorial(num - 1)   ' calling itself
   End If
End Function
```

I have used Doubles here because they can cope with very large numbers, and Factorial calculations can produce *very* large results. To test it, attach this code to a Button.

```
dim num, newnum As Double
num = InputBox("Enter number", "Factorial")
newnum = Factorial(num)
MsgBox(newnum)
```

3.12   Subs, functions and modules

Having created a useful sub or function, it seems a shame to have it restricted to one program, or to have to rewrite it (or copy it), into every program where you want to use it. There is a solution. If the code is written into a module, which is saved as a separate file, the file can be added into any other program later. Here's how.
- Start with the program containing either the Factorial or the Degree function.
- Use **Project > Add Module**. A new code window, entitled *Module1.bas*, will open. Copy the whole of the sub across to the module, using the Project window to move between the two.
- With the module window active, use **File | Save** xxx **As**, to save the Basic module to disk. Call it *fact.bas* or *degree.bas*, as appropriate.
- Close down the project and open a new one, or another existing project.
- Pull in the basic module, with **Project > Add File**. Write a short piece of code that will call the function, to check that it is there and working for you.

Any one Basic file can be added to as many different programs as you like, but remember that any changes you make to the file will affect every program in which it is used. As one Basic module can have any number of subs and functions within it, you could write all your general purpose functions in the one file, and add this to your programs.

You must also bear in mind that if the code contains references to controls, it will only work when used with programs that have controls of the same type and name.

3.13   Exercises

3.1   Take the `ElseIf` example routine from page 43 and rewrite it as a set of single line `If` structures. Note that the branch handled there by the `ElseIf` clause will need a compound `AND` test.

3.2   Write a program using two nested `For ... Next` loops to produce one of these patterns:

```
* 1                        8 ********
** 2                       7 *******
*** 3                      6 ******
**** 4                     5 *****
***** 5                    4 ****
****** 6                   3 ***
******* 7                  2 **
******** 8                 1 *
```

3.3   Design and write a times tables tester. It should ask the users what table they want to be tested on, then set a series of random problems from that table. If a user gets an answer wrong, the program should show the table before asking the next question.

Hint: Random numbers can be produced by the Rnd() function. This generates decimal fractions in the range 0 to 1. Multiply this by 10 to move the range on to 0 to 9.999, and use the Int() function to convert the result to an integer. The random number line should read something like:

```
x = Int(Rnd() * 10) + 1
```

The times table should be written into a RichTextBox, or a TextBox with its **Multiline** property set to *True*.

3.4   A health and fitness club has four levels of membership charges, based on the age of the member. 0–16 (Juniors) and 55–80 (Seniors) are both charged at half the 17–54 (Adult) rate of £250 p.a. Members aged 81 or over (Honorary) are allowed in free. Using a Select Case structure, write a program that will ask for the member's age, and display the membership category and charges.

3.5   Write a function to calculate the volume of rectangular objects from their length, width and height.

Solutions to Exercises 3.1, 3.2 and 3.4 are given in the Appendix.

3.14   Solution to task 3.1

```
    Private Sub Button1_Click(ByVal sender As System.Object, ByVal e As
System.EventArgs) Handles Button1.Click
    Dim sex, title As String
    Dim age As Integer
    sex = InputBox("Enter sex (M/F)")
    age = InputBox("Enter age")
    If sex = "M" Then
       If age > 16 Then  title = "Mr" Else title = "Master"
          ' first nested If
    ElseIf sex = "F" Then
       If age > 16 Then                    ' start of second
          title = "Ms"
       Else
          title = "Miss"
       End If                              ' end of second
    Else
       MsgBox "Sex Unknown"
       title = "??"
    End If                                 ' end of outer If
    MsgBox ("Your form of address is " & title)
    End Sub
```

4 Interacting with the user

Part of the Windows philosophy is that applications should be user-friendly. With this in mind, its designers have provided menus, icons, Buttons, scroll bars and other tools to simplify the interaction with the user. These tools are available to us in Visual Basic, and we should make full use of them.

4.1 Collecting inputs

Sometimes keyboard entry – the only form of input available in traditional programming languages – is the most appropriate way to get data from the user. At other times you can make life easier for the users, and reduce the need for error-checking in your program, by asking them to select from a list, check an option, slide a scroll bar or click on a Button.

Explore the alternatives, and whenever you want input, consider which method will be simplest for the user. A Windows application should be intuitive to use, so take as your rule "if it feels right, it must be right."

4.2 MsgBoxes

We have already made use of the `InputBox` and `MsgBox` facilities briefly, but both have additional features that should not be overlooked. A `MsgBox` can be used for input as well as output, and its message can be reinforced by a bright symbol; default values can be set for `InputBoxes` and both can carry titles.

Outputs via the MsgBox statement

When used for output, `MsgBox` takes this form:

```
MsgBox (prompt, buttons, title)
```

The *prompt* and *title* are strings, and can be text (in quotes), variables, string functions or combinations of these, joined by ampersands (&). If you want the text to spread over more than one line, include the newline (ASCII 10) and carriage return (ASCII 13) in it. The simplest way to do this is with the predefined constant `vbCrLf`, which is equivalent to "Chr(13) & Chr(10)". (See example below.)

The *buttons* option controls the symbol that is shown, which buttons are present and which is the default. The option can be given as a number value or as a constant, e.g. to produce a simple Yes/No choice, you could use either of these expressions:

```
MsgBox("Really quit?", 4, "Quit")
MsgBox("Really quit?", MsgBoxStyle.YesNo, "Quit")
```

The constants are easy to use as the list of possibles is offered to you when you type a `Msgbox` expression. However, they only allow you to set one aspect of the MsgBox options. To set two or more at one time, you must use the typecode numbers, adding together to give a single value. For example, to get a warning symbol, **OK** and **Cancel** Buttons, with **Cancel** (the second button) set as the default, you would need the typecode **1 + 48 + 256**. This could be written into the statement as the expression **1+48+256**, or as the total **305**.

Typecodes

Button	Codes	Constants
OK	0	OKOnly
OK and Cancel	1	OKCancel
Abort, Retry and Ignore	2	AbortRetryIgnore
Yes, No and Cancel	3	YesNoCancel
Yes and No	4	YesNo
Retry and Cancel	5	RetryCancel

Symbols	Codes	Constants
None	0	
✖	16	Critical
?	32	Question
⚠	48	Exclamation
ⓘ	64	Information

Default Button	Codes	Constants
First	0	DefaultButton1
Second	256	DefaultButton2
Third	512	DefaultButton3

Where `MsgBox` is only being used for output, the Buttons are irrelevant, so the only valid *Buttons* options are 0, 16, 32, 48 and 64.

The box shown here was produced by the code given below. Note the use of the `vbCrLf` constant, that holds the linefeed and carriage return characters, to produce a two-line message, and the 64 typecode which gives the Information symbol. To test this, and later examples, type the code into a `Button_Click` Sub, then run the program and click the Button to watch them work.

```
Dim prompt, title As String
Dim StyleCode As Integer
prompt = "Prompt for the user " & vbCrLf & "A second line"
StyleCode = 64                              'info graphic
title = "Meaningful Title"
MsgBox (prompt, StyleCode, title)
```

Note

If no symbol is wanted, the buttons option can be omitted altogether – though if you do want to include a title, you must put in an extra comma, as the system expects the title to be the *third* item in the list, e.g.

```
MsgBox (message,,  title)
```

Inputs via the MsgBox function

If you want to collect a reply from a MsgBox, it must be used in its *function* form.

```
result = MsgBox(prompt, typecode, title)
```

This differs from the statement in that it returns a value, and this must be used or collected in a variable. The value shows which button was clicked.

Value	Button	Value	Button
1	OK	2	Cancel
3	Abort	4	Retry
5	Ignore	6	Yes
7	No		

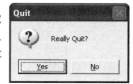

This box was defined with a typecode of 36, made up of 32 for the question mark and 4 to get the **Yes** and **No** buttons. You will see that it has been written in the code as 32 + 4. It could equally well have been written as a simple 36.

Here's the code:

```
Dim typecode As Integer
Dim reply As Integer
typecode = 32 + 4                              ' ? and Yes/No
reply = MsgBox("Really Quit? ", typecode, "Quit")
If reply = 6 Then End                          ' 6 = "Yes"
```

Task 4.1

Add a confirmation MsgBox, with OK and Cancel, to any program with a Quit Button. It should carry the exclamation mark and the two-line message:

```
Quit selected.
Please Confirm
```

The code should only end the program if OK is selected.

4.3   InputBoxes

An `InputBox` can only ever be used in this (function) form:

result = InputBox(*prompt, title, default_value*)

Unlike `MsgBox`, `InputBox` does not take a typecode. It will always display **OK** and **Cancel**, and cannot hold symbols. The *default_value* is a string that can be displayed in the entry slot of the box, and will be returned if the user presses **OK**. In the example below, "-99", which is being used to mark the end of the routine, has been set as the default.

Clicking **Cancel**, or pressing **[Esc]**, produces a *Null* value, which can cause problems – trying to copy this into a number variable would cause an error. If you want to use `InputBox` to get a number, the safe solution is to take the input value into a string, and check that something is there before passing it to the number variable.

To run the next example, type this code into a `Button_Click` sub.

```
Private Sub Button1_Click(ByVal sender As System.Object, ByVal e As
System.EventArgs) Handles Button1.Click
   Dim prompt, title As String
   Dim reply As String
   Dim numval, total As Single
   Do
      prompt = "Enter a number or -99 to quit"
      title = "Adder"
      reply = InputBox(prompt, title, "-99")
      If reply = "-99" Then
         Exit Do
      Else
         If reply >= "0" And reply <= "9" Then numval = Val(reply)
Else numval = 0
         total = total + numval
      End If
      MsgBox("Total so far " & total)
   Loop Until numval = -99
End Sub
```

Figure 4.1

An InputBox
displaying a
default value

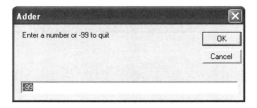

4.4 ScrollBars

ScrollBars are familiar to any Windows user and offer a convenient way of controlling a value that can vary between fixed limits. They could be used, for example, for setting the Red, Blue and Green values when defining colours (see Chapter 8), but are an interesting alternative to keyboard input in many situations.

ScrollBars have five key properties:

Value　　　　the position of the slider in relation to the ends

Min　　　　　the value when the slider is at the top, or left, of the bar

Max　　　　　the value when the slider is at the bottom, or right, of the bar

SmallChange　the result of clicking on an arrow

LargeChange　the result of clicking on the bar beside the slider.

All values must be within the normal integer range, i.e.0 to +32,767, though in practice your Max is likely to be much tighter than that.

The next example uses ScrollBars to move a block around the screen – and the whole program contains only three lines of code! To try it, place these objects on a new form.

Vertical ScrollBar, down the left side

Horizontal ScrollBar, along the bottom

Panel, of a size that will fit within the limits of the scroll bars

PictureBox, named *picBlock*, placed within the Frame

Button, captioned "Quit".

The purpose of the Panel is to provide a running area for the Block. Any object placed within a Panel cannot be moved out of it, and its Top and Left co-ordinates will be relative to the Panel, not to the Form beneath.

As the Panel's size is the same as the ScrollBars' Max values, we have a simple translation of ScrollBar values to Block co-ordinates. The Panel should be aligned as closely as possible with the ends of the ScrollBars, inside the Arrow Buttons. The Max value of the VScrollBar control should be the same as the Height of the Frame, and the Max of the HScrollBar the same as the Panel's Width.

The Block merely needs to be visible on screen, and that can be achieved by setting the BackColor to a distinctive colour. Make sure that you place it within the Panel when you first define it.

For the code, go to the procedures listed here and type the single lines in each.

```
Private Sub HScrollBar1_Scroll(ByVal sender As System.Object, ByVal e
As System.Windows.Forms.ScrollEventArgs) Handles HScrollBar1.Scroll
   picBlock.Left = HScrollBar1.Value
End Sub


Private Sub VScrollBar1_Scroll(ByVal sender As System.Object, ByVal
e As System.Windows.Forms.ScrollEventArgs) Handles VScrollBar1.Scroll
   picBlock.Top = VScrollBar1.Value
End Sub
```

Figure 4.2

The screen display of the
ScrollBar testing program

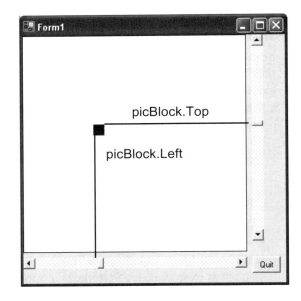

```
      Private Sub btnQuit_Click(ByVal sender As System.Object, ByVal e
   As System.EventArgs) Handles btnQuit.Click
      End
   End Sub
```

4.5 GroupBoxes

A GroupBox by itself does very little. The chief purpose of this control is to enclose
other objects, providing a sort of form within a form. Probably their most common
use is to hold sets of RadioButtons or CheckBoxes, as you will see below. Another
sensible use for them is to enclose Labels and TextBoxes where the Label serves
as a prompt for input into the TextBox.

When a GroupBox is made visible or invisible, all the objects within it appear
or disappear; when it is moved, they all move with it. The latter is very useful at
design time, and possibly during the execution of a program.

4.6 RadioButtons

The RadioButtons controls are almost always used in sets, and only one can be
selected at any one time. This means that you cannot have more than one set of
options on one form – you may have placed them as separate sets, but the system
will treat them as one. The solution is to place your RadioButtons within
GroupBoxes, as each grouped set is treated separately. These provide a nice visual
touch to the display as well as being essential to the grouping of RadioButtons.

There are essentially two ways of finding out which RadioButton has been
selected.

The first is to use the RadioButton's **Checked** property. If a RadioButton has been selected, it will be *True*. You can therefore use expressions such as:

```
If RadioButton2.Checked Then...
```

and the statements that follow this test will only be executed if *RadioButton2* has been selected. This is probably the best approach where there are only two possible choices, as it leads to a neat `If ... Then ... Else ...` structure.

The alternative is to set a variable when the RadioButton is clicked. This is more suitable where there are a number of possible options, and is the approach that has been used in the following example. It deals, appropriately enough, with options, though the options in this case are subject choices.

A student must choose one language, from Option Block 1, and one creative subject, from Option Block 2. Each block is represented by a GroupBox on the form, and the RadioButtons should be suitably named.

The variables *Choice1* and *Choice2* are used to collect the choices, and are declared at the top of the form so that they are available to every sub. Values are assigned to these variables when the RadioButtons are clicked. When the *Show Choice* Button is clicked, their current values should be displayed in the TextBox.

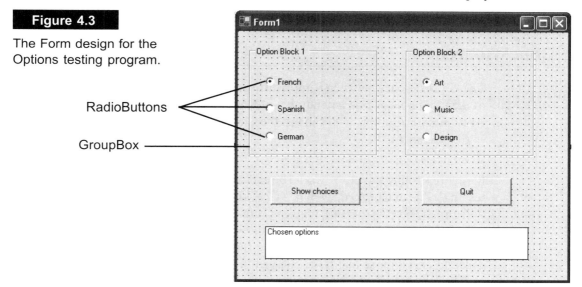

Figure 4.3

The Form design for the Options testing program.

RadioButtons

GroupBox

Each RadioButton's `CheckChanged` sub follows this pattern:

```
Private Sub rdoFrench_CheckedChanged(ByVal sender As System.Object,
ByVal e As System.EventArgs) Handles rdoFrench.CheckedChanged
    choice1 = "French"
End Sub
```

The defaults are French and Art. These are set at design time, by selecting *True* for their Checked property. If the Checked was to be used directly in the program, no further action would be needed. As we are handling the selection through variables, we must also set default values for them. This can be done in the `Form_Load` sub – double-click anywhere on the form to get into this sub.

```
    Private Sub Form1_Load(ByVal sender As System.Object, ByVal e As
System.EventArgs) Handles MyBase.Load
    choice1 = "French"
    choice2 = "Art"
End Sub
```

The *Show Choices* Button needs code like this:

```
    Private Sub btnShow_Click(ByVal sender As System.Object, ByVal e
As System.EventArgs) Handles btnShow.Click
    lblChoices.Text = "Block 1 = " & choice1 & vbCrLf & "Block 2 = " &
choice2
End Sub
```

> ### Task 4.2
>
> Set up a form to the design shown above. Name the OptionButtons to match
> their captions, starting each name with *opt* to show that this is an OptionButton
> control. Attach to the OptionButtons and the Form the code discussed above,
> plus a procedure on Show Choices to display the student's choices.

4.7   CheckBoxes

The key difference between **RadioButtons** and **CheckBoxes**, apart from the shape
of their symbols, is that any number of CheckBoxes in a set may be *True* at once.
As with RadioButtons, you can test the Checked property of a CheckBox directly.
In the statement:

```
    If CheckBox1.Checked Then ...
```

the actions following `Then` would be executed if Checked was True. And you *must*
test the value of Checked, even in a CheckBox's `CheckChanged` sub, for clicking
will turn the box On *and* Off, toggling between the two states. This is different from
a RadioButton, where a click always turns it on.

In the Xmas list example shown here, the user is offered a choice of presents and
asked to check those that he or she would like.

The variable *gifts* is used as a counter, and increased by 1 each time a CheckBox
is turned on. When the *Done* Button is pressed, the code will display a different
message, depending upon the greed of the user.

The Checked property of a CheckBox is changed as soon as it is clicked, and
before the system gets to the `CheckChanged` sub. Knowing this, we can write code
for those subs that will add to the *gifts* count if the box is checked and subtract if
the click has turned it off.

```
    Private Sub chkDosh_CheckedChanged(ByVal sender As System.Object,
ByVal e As System.EventArgs) Handles chkDosh.CheckedChanged
    If checkDosh.Checked Then gifts += 1 Else gifts -= 1
End Sub
```

Figure 4.4

Use CheckBoxes where more than one option can be selected

Code is easier to understand if you name controls after their captions.

These CheckBoxes might be named chkHiFi, chkDosh, chkFerrari, chkRolex, and chkTeddy.

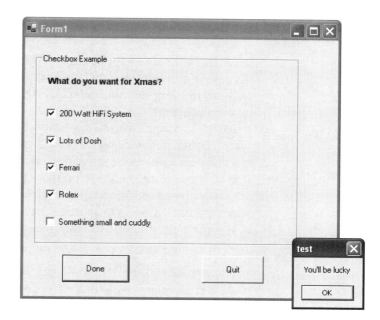

In this simple example, the code on the **Done** Button concentrates on the *gifts* total and largely ignores the states of the individual CheckBoxes. (Note the special message that is given to those who only want a teddy!) In practice, any program which used CheckBoxes would also want to react to their specific values.

```
    Private Sub btnDone_Click(ByVal sender As System.Object, ByVal e
As System.EventArgs) Handles btnDone.Click
    Dim message As String
    If gifts > 3 Then
       message = "You'll be lucky"
    ElseIf gifts = 1 And chkTeddy.Checked Then
       message = "Aah, bless!"
    Else
       message = "Write to Santa"
    End If
    MsgBox(message)
End Sub
```

Task 4.3

Complete the example program, building on the code given above. The *gifts* variable should be declared at the top of the form.

4.8 Menus

Look at any Windows application and you will see that it has a menu system. Why? Because it is the simplest and clearest way of showing your users the full range of facilities in your program, and of giving access to those facilities. Creating a menu is straightforward.

To add a menu bar to an application, drop a **MainMenu** control onto the form – don't bother about trying to locate it carefully as it knows where to go. There are two visible results: at the top of the form you will see a menu bar, blank apart from a grey "Type Here" message on the left; and a tray appears at the bottom of the workspace, with the MainMenu component placed on it.

There are three aspects to setting up a menu system:

- Creating the structure of main menus and submenus;
- Setting the names, options and other properties of the items;
- Writing the code to be activated by the menu choices.

If you were writing a simple word processor – as we will do in Chapter 7 – you would need a **File** menu with options such as **New**, **Open**, **Save**, **Print** and **Exit**, a **Format** menu, a **Help** menu and perhaps others. You can see such a menu system under construction here.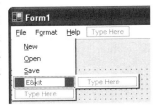

Building a menu structure

A new heading or item for a menu can be added wherever you see "Type Here".

When typing the menu entries, one of the letters – usually the first – should be set so that it is underlined and can be selected by the **[Alt]**+ key combination. To do this, type an ampersand (&) before it. When you move on to the next item, the & will disappear and the letter will be underlined. *Watch out for duplication! You cannot use the same selecting letter twice in the same menu.*

- **To start a new main menu:** type the heading in the menu bar. A new "Type Here" will appear beside it (for the next main heading) and below it (for a menu item).

- **To add an item to a menu:** type below the existing items.

- **To start a new submenu:** select the entry that leads to the submenu then type the first item in the "Type Here" to its right.

- **To insert a separator line:** right-click on the item below where the separator is to go, then select **Insert Separator** from the pop-up menu.

- **To edit a menu entry:** click on it once to select it, then again to place the typing cursor into it and edit as normal.

- **To move a menu entry:** click on it and drag it to its new position.

- **To stop work on the menus:** click anywhere else on the form.

- **To restart work on the menus:** click on any heading in the menu bar.

Setting properties

At this stage you have the shape of the menus and the text for the entries, but little else. Each item has been allocated a name such as *MenuItem1*, *MenuItem2*, etc., and these should be renamed to identify them clearly. To rename a menu item:

1 Select the item on the menu.

2 Locate the **Name** field in the **Properties** window.

3 Replace the allocated name with a meaningful one.

While you are at the Properties window, you can also set the options. There are two key ones to note:

- **Checked** puts a tick by the entry, to show that an on/off option is on.

- **RadioCheck** puts a round bullet by the entry, to show that this is the chosen option from the set.

These options should be set to True at design time, if the default settings are on. Otherwise they can be set during run-time.

Adding code

When the user selects a menu item, whether by clicking or using an **[Alt]**+ key combination, it triggers a `Click` event. The menu command's code could be written directly there, but if you want to be able to activate the same command from a toolbar Button – and we do with many of ours – it is better to write the code in a separate subroutine. In this case, the item's `Click` event simply calls the subroutine, e.g. a **File > New** command might lead to this:

```
    Private Sub FileNewCheck_Click(ByVal sender As System.Object,
ByVal e As System.EventArgs) Handles FileNewCheck.Click
    newFile()
End Sub
```

4.9 Context menus

A context menu is built in almost the same way as a main menu. The main differences are that the menu must be linked to an object and there can only be one main list of options. To create a context menu:

1 Select the **ContextMenu** control from the Toolbox – you will find it towards the bottom of the Windows Forms set.

2 Drop the control anywhere on the form. The component will appear on the tray at the bottom, and the prompt 'Context Menu' will temporarily replace any existing headings in the menu bar.

Figure 4.5

Starting to edit a
context menu

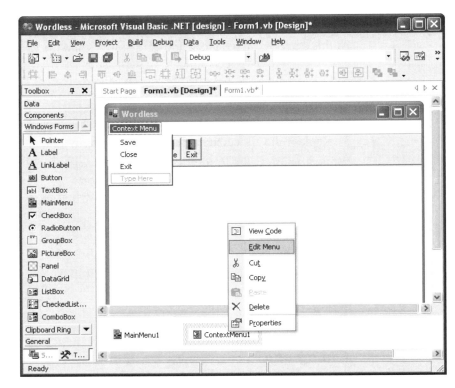

Figure 4.5

Starting to edit a
context menu

3   Add your menu items – starting submenus if required – in the 'Type Here'
    prompts.

4   Set the names and other properties, and add code as for ordinary menu items.

5   Click anywhere off the menu when you have done. The main menu headings
    will reappear.

- If you need to edit the context menu later, click on its icon or label in the
  component band. The menu will again replace the main menu. Right-click on
  the label and select **Edit Menu**, or click directly
  into the displayed menu.

6   Select the control that the context menu is to
    pop-up from.

7   In the **Properties** window, click into the
    ContextMenu field, drop down its options and
    select the context menu.

- If you want context menus on a number of components, you can create a new menu for each
  (the simple solution) or set up one 'dynamic'
  menu where the contents alter to suit the selected
  control. Look up dynamic context menus in the
  Help system if you want to pursue this approach.

4.10   Toolbars

Toolbars are unexpectedly different from menus in the way that they are created and used. This is probably because a toolbar is a single item, and its Buttons are segments within it – while on a menu, each entry is a separate item, and the structure is a container to hold them. You can see this when you set up the toolbar, but it is also clear when you come to add code – there is only one **Click** event for the whole toolbar. All tool Button clicks lead to the same place, so you have to write code to identify which Button has been clicked, before you can respond to it.

It shows up again in the way that toolbar icons are managed. Tools do not have their own Image property. Instead, there is a separate ImageList, and each tool is linked to a numbered item in this list. You can set up the ImageList first, or build a text-only toolbar and add the images later. We'll start with text, so that we can get our heads around toolbars before we worry about making them pretty.

To create a toolbar:

1   Select the **Toolbar** control from the Toolbox and drop it onto the form. It will automatically locate itself just below the menu bar.

2   Select **Buttons** in the Toolbar's Properties window and click .... The ToolBarButton Collection Editor will open.

3   Click **Add**. The first Button will appear in the **Members:** list.

4   Type the **Text** to be displayed on the Button, and the **ToolTip Text**, if required.

5   Repeat steps **3** and **4** to add the other Buttons.

6   Click **OK** to close the Collection Editor window.

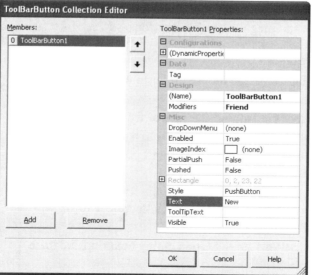

Figure 4.6

The Collection Editor as the first button is being defined

Properties of individual toolbar buttons are accessed through the Collection Editor

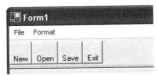

Figure 4.7

The toolbar, waiting
for its images

The default toolbar Button style is **PushButton**, but there are three other options
in the **Style** field:

- **ToggleButton**, makes it into an on/off switch. If you want to signify that it is
  on at the start, set Pushed to True.
- **Separator** creates a gap between the Buttons.
- **DropDownButton** attaches a drop-down list to the Button. The list is created
  in a context menu, which is linked to the Button by selecting it in the
  DropDownMenu field.

Images for icons

Before you can put an image list together, you need to find or create the images.
You can create your own using the Visual Studio Image Editor (or any graphics
package that can produce .bmp files) – though it may make you appreciate the
design skills that have gone into other people's icons. The ideal image should be
a clear reminder of the purpose of the Button, it should look good and you must be
able to draw with a 16×16 grid of dots! If it is the right size and different from the
other Button images, that will do. (See page 70 for more on the Image Editor.)

   If you want to get your image list started quickly, there are some standard
images for the filing, and the cut and paste commands, tucked away deep in the
Visual Studio folder. The exact location will depend upon your system, but it
should be something like:

   C:\Program Files\Microsoft Visual Studio .NET 2003\SDK\v1.1\ QuickStart\
winforms\samples\controlreference\tooltipctl\vb

If you can't find the folder down this path, you can locate it by running a search for
one of its images – try looking for *clsdfold.bmp* (the Closed Folder image).

ImageLists

Creating an image list is similar to creating a toolbar
– this is another collection.

1 Select the **ImageList** control from the Toolbox –
   you will find it just below the RichTextBox.

2 Drop it onto the form – it will go into the component tray.

3 Locate the **Images** field in the Properties window
   and click .... The **Image Collection Editor** window will open.

4 Click **Add**. At the **Open** dialog box, find and open
   the first file.

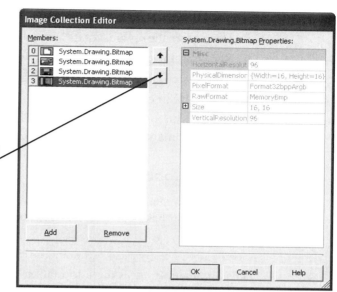

Figure 4.8

The Image Collection Editor with four images in place

The images are easier to handle if they are in the same order as the buttons – use the arrows to adjust them as necessary.

5 Repeat step **4** to add as many images as needed for the toolbar.

6 Click **OK** to close the Editor.

Linking images to toolbar buttons

The final stage of creating the toolbar is to link the images to the Buttons. This is done through the Toolbar control.

1 Select the toolbar and go to the **Properties** window.

2 Click into the **ImageList** field and select your newly-created ImageList from its drop-down list.

3 Click on the **Buttons** field to open the ToolBarButtons Collection Editor.

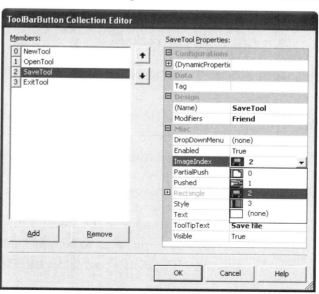

Figure 4.9

Allocating images to buttons in the ToolbarButton Collection Editor

4 Click on a tool in the **Members:** list.

5 Drop down the options for its **ImageIndex** property – this links to the ImageList.

6 Select an image.

7 Repeat steps **4** to **6** as required.

8 Click **OK** to close the Editor.

A toolbar with images in places – all of these except for the Exit image are from the supplied set.

Code for toolbars

As you will remember, a toolbar has only one `Click` event. How then do you know which Button has been clicked? The answer lies in this parameter of the `Click` event:

…ByVal e As System.Windows.Forms.ToolBarButtonClickEventArgs…

The argument *e* stores the information generated by the `Click` event. The most important part of this is in the `Button` property, which identifies the Button that was clicked. The expression:

```
ToolBar1.Buttons.IndexOf(e.Button)
```

gives the number of the Button, counting from 0. That can then be used in an `If…Then…` or `Select Case…` structure to direct the flow to the appropriate code. Here's the toolbar's Click event sub, in skeleton form. The *'new routine* and similar comments will be replaced by code later.

```
Private Sub tBar1_ButtonClick(ByVal sender As System.Object,ByVal e As
System.Windows.Forms.ToolBarButtonClickEventArgs) Handles tBar1.ButtonClick
    Select Case  ToolBar1.Buttons.IndexOf(e.Button)
        Case 0 :    ' new routine
        Case 1 :    ' open routine
        Case 2 :    ' save routine
        Case 3 :    ' exit routine
    End Select
End Sub
```

4.11 The Image Editor

Visual Studio has its own Image Editor. This is not a high-level graphics package – it has the same kind of facilities as Windows Paint, which is a certainly enough for creating icon images. Try it out. This is an optional extra – if you prefer to use other graphics software, then please do so.

To create an icon image in the Image Editor:

1 Open the **File** menu, point to **New** and select **File**.

2 At the **New File** dialog box, select **Bitmap File** as the type.

Figure 4.10

Drawing a toolbar
button image in
Image Editor. The
tools on the toolbar
and the Image
menu are almost
identical to those of
Paint. Experiment –
you'll soon get the
hang of them.

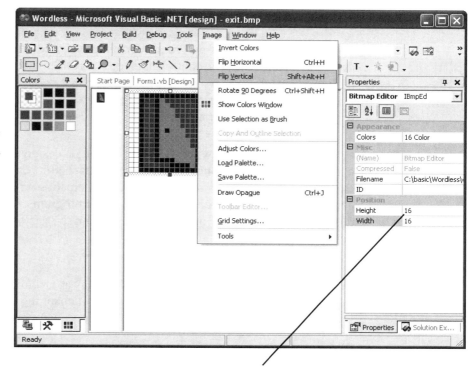

Set the image size in the Properties window

3 The Image Editor will open in the main workspace, with a new toolbar above
it and a palette on the far left. You will also note that there is now an **Image**
menu. If the toolbar does not appear, right-click on any blank space in the
toolbar area and tick **Image Editor** in the list that appears.

4 The default image size is 48 × 48 pixels. Change this to 16 × 16 in the Properties window.

5 Create your image, using the 'life-size' copy on the left as a guide to how it
really looks.

The tools are almost identical to those of Paint, but note that the third Button
from the right line holds the options for line thickness or drawing style of all
tools.

You are limited to 16 colours, but you can define them yourself. Double-click
on a colour in the palette to edit it.

6 When you are finished, use **File > Save Bitmap As...** to save the image for
use in your image list. Leave the file type at the default .bmp – the .gif and .jpg
save options are there in case you want to produce images for web pages.

4.12 Worked example

This is an arithmetic test program, where the type and difficulty of the problems can be set by the user. The controls include a ScrollBar, a set of OptionButtons and a Menu, as well as others covered in earlier chapters. In its code you will find a `Select Case` and a variety of `If` structures.

• Another point to note here is how the values held by some of the controls are treated as variables.

It is not possible to draw a straightforward JSP design for the program as the operations are split among the procedures attached to controls, and the flow of execution is largely dependent on the user's interaction with the controls. The best approach with this, as with most Visual Basic programs, is to start with the form design and to look at the actions that arise from the use of the controls.

Form design

For this program we want a form that will display an arithmetic problem and accept and check an answer. It should have a means of changing the type of sum and the level of difficulty, and should display the score. A layout is shown in Figure 4.11.

Controls and Events

• **lblNum1** and **lblNum2** are Labels to hold numbers generated at random.

• **lblSumtype** is a Label that holds the symbol for the type of sum.

• **txtAnswer** is a TextBox – the only control into which the user can type.

• **grpType** is a GroupBox that contains four RadioButtons, named **rdoAdd, rdoSub, rdoTimes** and **rdoDiv**. Code attached to their **Click** events will change *lblSumtype*'s Text.

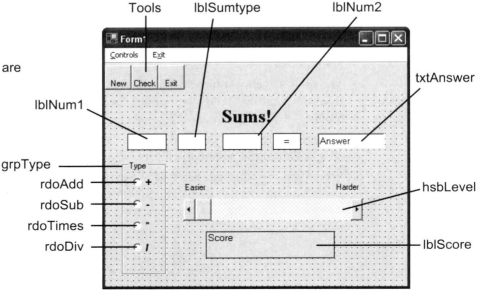

Figure 4.11

The form design – unnamed controls are purely decorative.

- **hsbLevel** is a Horizontal Scroll Bar that sets the level of difficulty. When a new problem is generated, its value determines the scale of the numbers:

```
level = Val(hsbLevel.Value)
n1 = Int(Rnd() * level) + 1
```

  Its limits are the Min and Max properties which are set at design time. If the program is intended for use by young children, the limits might be set at 5 and 10; for older users, armed with calculators, they might be 10 to 100 or more.

- **lblScore** is a Label to display the score and is updated by the checking code. The variables that count the number of problems and of correct answers must be declared at the top of the form so that they are generally available.

Menu commands

These replicate the effects of the controls on the form. Though this is unnecessary, you will often find similar situations in Windows application programs. It takes very little code to offer menu, keystroke and toolbar or Button alternatives to activate the same command, but it does give your users the choice. Some people like to pick their way through menus, others prefer a quick click on the screen. We are using menus, Buttons and a toolbar here to give practice in all three.

The menu structure is:

Menu Option	**Comment**
Controls	Header
New Problem	= Toolbar Button0
Check Answer	= Toolbar Button1
Type of Sum	Header
Add	= rdoAdd_Click
Subtract	= rdoSub_Click
Times	= rdoTimes_Click
Divide	= rdoDiv_Click
Exit	Header
Yes	End program
No	Does nothing

The toolbar

The example developed here has only three Buttons: **New**, **Check** and **End**. When clicked, these will run the subs to generate a new problem, check the answer and exit from the program. I have left them as text-only; you can add images if you like.

Coding

Much of the code flows naturally from the specifications of the controls, with a little more detailed design needed for a couple of larger routines.

General variables and default values

You need generally accessible variables to store the correct answer (*Ans*), the count of right answers (*rtans*) and the count of questions (*qcount*). These should be declared these variables at the top of the code, above the first sub.

Their initial values should be set in the `Form_Load` sub. The default type of sum and level of difficulty should also be set at this point.

Generating a new problem

This procedure takes the shape:

```
Generate two random numbers
store them in n1 & n2
display them in lblNum1 & lblNum2
Work out the correct answer, storing it in the variable Ans
   The calculation to depend upon the character in lblSumtype
Clear txtAnswer and place the cursor ready for the response
```

We need to be able to run this operation from both the menu command and the toolbar Button. The simplest solution is to create a free-standing sub to handle the operation, and call that from the command or the Button, with the line:

```
NewProblem()
```

which calls up the **NewProblem** sub.

Has [Enter] been pressed?

The answer must be checked. We are offering our user a Check Answer Button and a menu option, but we should also run the check automatically after an **[Enter]** keypress that will tell us that he or she has finished typing the answer. We are going to have to dig into the parameters to do this.

The `KeyPress` code has an `e` parameter which holds the `KeyPressEventArgs`. Within this is `KeyChar`, which holds the character that was last pressed. In this case we are looking for **[Enter]** which is Chr(13). That gives us this code:

```
If e.KeyChar = Chr(13) Then CheckAnswer()
```

Note that `KeyPress` is not the default event for a TextBox. To open this sub in the Code window, select **txtAnswer** from the Class Name drop-down list, on the left above the code, and then **KeyPress** from the Method Name list on the right.

Answer checking

The design of the checking code is straightforward:

```
get the value from the answer box
if the answer is correct
   increase the score
else display the correct answer
increase the question count
display the current score and count
```

In the correct answer and the score display we can use either + or & as a concatenator to join the variables and the accompanying text. It is not necessary to convert the numbers to strings first.

```
"The correct answer was " & Ans
```

As we need to be able to run this code from three different start points, it should be written into a free-standing sub. I've called it *CheckAnswer()*.

Changing the SumType

Users can change the SumType either by clicking a RadioButton or through the menu. Whichever route they choose, the operation takes only simple lines like this:

```
lblSumType.Text = "+"
```

As there is so little code, it's not a problem to duplicate it in both the menu command and the Button.

Random numbers

The Rnd() function produces a fractional value in the range of 0 to 1. It is pseudo-random – i.e. every value is as likely as every other, and you cannot predict what will come next, but it is actually the result of a complex calculation. Values such as 0.4162738746 are rarely much use in a program, but they can easily be converted into more useful ones by expressions following this pattern:

```
num = Int(Rnd * range) + base
```

If you want numbers in the range 1 to 6, for a Dice simulator, the line would be:

```
num = Int(Rnd * 6) + 1
```

The *base* number is necessary as Int() truncates values – it chops off the decimal part, leaving just the integer.

Figure 4.12

The program in action – here an answer has just been checked

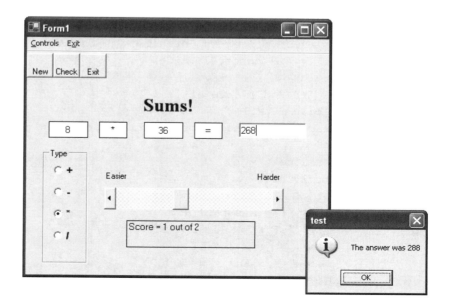

Look what happens with these values:

Rnd	Rnd * 6	Int (Rnd * 6)	Int (Rnd * 6) + 1
0.54	3.24	3	4
0.05	0.30	0	1
0.90	5.40	5	6

The calculation that produces random numbers always works through the same sequence, but this is so complex that you cannot predict the next number, as long as you start at a different place each time. To make the system select a new start point, based on the system's clock, place this statement in the Form_Load code:

```
Randomize ()
```

The Sums code

```
Public Class Form1
   Inherits  System.Windows.Forms.Form
   Dim Ans As Integer              'declare general variables
   Dim rtans As Integer
   Dim qcount As Integer
+ Windows Form Designer generated code
   Private Sub Form1_Load(ByVal sender As System.Object, ByVal e As
System.EventArgs) Handles MyBase.Load
   Randomize()
   qcount = 0
   rtans = 0
   lblSumType.Text = "+"
   hsbLevel.Value = 10
End Sub

Private Sub NewProblem()
   Dim level, n1, n2 As Integer
   level = Val(hsbLevel.Value)
   n1 = Int(Rnd() * level) + 1
   n2 = Int(Rnd() * level) + 1
   If lblSumType.Text = "/" Then n1 *= n2
   'ensures that the numbers will divide evenly

   lblNum1.Text = n1
   lblNum2.Text = n2
   Select Case lblSumType.Text
      Case "+": Ans = n1 + n2
      Case "-" : Ans = n1 - n2
      Case "*" : Ans = n1 * n2
      Case "/" : Ans = n1 / n2
   End Select
```

```
     txtAnswer.Text = ""
     txtAnswer.Focus()
     qcount += 1
  End Sub

 Private Sub CheckAnswer()
    Dim userAnswer As Integer
    userAnswer = Val(txtAnswer.Text)
    If userAnswer = Ans Then
      MsgBox("Correct")
      rtans += 1
    Else
      MsgBox("The answer was " & Ans, MsgBoxStyle.Information)
    End If
    lblScore.Text = "Score = " & rtans & " out of " & qcount
  End Sub

    Private Sub rdoAdd_CheckedChanged(ByVal sender As System.Object,
ByVal e As System.EventArgs) Handles rdoAdd.CheckedChanged
    lblSumType.Text = "+"
  End Sub

    Private Sub rdoSub_CheckedChanged(ByVal sender As System.Object,
ByVal e As System.EventArgs) Handles rdoSub.CheckedChanged
    lblSumType.Text = "-"
  End Sub

    Private Sub rdoTimes_CheckedChanged(ByVal sender As System.Object,
ByVal e As System.EventArgs) Handles rdoTimes.CheckedChanged
    lblSumType.Text = "*"
  End Sub

    Private Sub rdoDiv_CheckedChanged(ByVal sender As System.Object,
ByVal e As System.EventArgs) Handles rdoDiv.CheckedChanged
    lblSumType.Text = "/"
  End Sub

    Private Sub menuNewProblem_Click(ByVal sender As System.Object,
ByVal e As System.EventArgs) Handles menuNewProblem.Click
    NewProblem()
  End Sub

    Private Sub menuCheckAnswer_Click(ByVal sender As System.Object,
ByVal e As System.EventArgs) Handles menuCheckAnswer.Click
    CheckAnswer()
  End Sub

    Private Sub menuAdd_Click(ByVal sender As System.Object, ByVal e
As System.EventArgs)
    lblSumType.Text = "+"
  End Sub
```

```
   Private Sub menuSub_Click(ByVal sender As System.Object, ByVal e
As System.EventArgs)
   lblSumType.Text = "-"
End Sub
   Private Sub menuTimes_Click(ByVal sender As System.Object, ByVal e
As System.EventArgs)
   lblSumType.Text = "*"
End Sub
   Private Sub menuDiv_Click(ByVal sender As System.Object, ByVal e
As System.EventArgs)
   lblSumType.Text = "/"
End Sub
   Private Sub MenuExitYes_Click(ByVal sender As System.Object, ByVal
e As System.EventArgs) Handles MenuExitYes.Click
   End
End Sub
   Private Sub txtAnswer_KeyPress(ByVal sender As Object, ByVal e As
System.Windows.Forms.KeyPressEventArgs) Handles txtAnswer.KeyPress
   If e.KeyChar = Chr(13) Then CheckAnswer()
End Sub
   Private Sub ToolBar1_ButtonClick(ByVal sender As System.Object,
ByVal e As System.Windows.Forms.ToolBarButtonClickEventArgs) Handles
ToolBar1.ButtonClick
   Select Case ToolBar1.Buttons.IndexOf(e.Button)
      Case 0 : NewProblem()
      Case 1 : CheckAnswer()
      Case 2 : End
   End Select
End Sub
End Class
```

4.13   Exercises

4.1   Design and write a program that could be used for the analysis of a simple questionnaire. This should only ask a single question, with a fixed set of possible answers – something along the lines of "What do you think of the canteen food? (A) Great value for money, (B) Good, (C) Fair, (D) Poor, (E) I'd rather starve."

Use a set of Options and Buttons marked *Next*, *Display Totals* and *Quit*. When the *Next* Button is clicked, your code should scan the Options, add 1 to the appropriate total and clear the Options ready for the next response. Display Totals should produce a display of the question and the scores of the replies.

4.2 Use the Image Editor to create suitable icons then add them to the toolbar in the Sums program.

4.3 Write a program to give a simple demonstration of Options, CheckBoxes, InputBoxes, MsgBoxes. The options should be selected from a Menu, so a separate demonstration for Menus will not be needed.

Hint: To keep the screen display clean and simple at runtime, turn off the Visible property of the Panels, GroupBoxes, Labels and other controls that you will use in your various demonstrations. They can then be turned back on when a particular demonstration is selected, and off when it ends.

A possible solution to Exercise 4.1 is given in the Appendix. The others are too open-ended – if they look OK, and do what is needed, then they must be right!

5 Testing and debugging

Even the best programmers make mistakes! Fortunately, the Visual Studio provides excellent tools for finding and correcting errors.

5.1 Errors and error spotting

There are three main categories of error.

- **Syntax errors** are mistakes in the way that the language is used – typically misspelling keywords, giving the wrong type of data to a function, or missing out part of a command. These are usually spotted by the system, either when you move the cursor off the line or when it builds the program.

- **Logical errors** occur when you use the words and structures correctly, but don't quite manage to say what you mean. Visual Basic has no means of identifying these, and unless the error crashes the program or produces visibly strange results, you will not be aware of them yourself. Commercial software is all too often released with bugs that only show up when the programs are pushed to their limits by users. To ensure that you have found and cured all logical errors, you must design a thorough testing procedure that will explore every possible route through the program, and every possible combination of values. Any problems thrown up by the testing can then be investigated using the debugging tools.

- **Runtime errors** can occur because of unexpected external events, e.g. the user inputs the wrong type of data, or the program attempts to load a non-existent file or communicate with a detached peripheral. You cannot prevent these, but you can prevent them from crashing your program.

Scanning for errors

When you are writing your code, as soon as you press [Enter] at the end of the line, or move the cursor off it, the line is scanned for errors. If one is found, it is given a wavy blue underline. Point at it and a pop-up box will tell you what's wrong. This will usually point out missing keywords or other punctuation, but will sometimes give a less-than-helpful 'Syntax error' message.

If no errors are found, the line is rewritten in a standard format. Spaces are inserted around symbols, and those words that the system recognises as being part of the Visual Basic vocabulary are forced into mixed upper and lower case and recoloured.

Do check the revised line. A misspelt keyword will occasionally fail to produce an error message, because the system assumes you mean something entirely different. If a word has not been reformatted, first check its spelling, then check your quotes. One or other will almost certainly be the cause of the problem.

Compile-time error reports

The line scan will pick up errors on individual lines and check the syntax of **If**, **Case**, **Loop** or similar structures, though it may not always pick up errors in more complex structures. The ones that the scanner missed or that you failed to notice will be picked up when the Studio attempts to build the project.

If you see this:

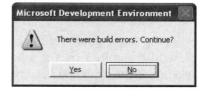

Click **No** to return to the Code window. At the bottom of the window you will see a panel listing the errors. These are usually identified by line number – and line numbers are not normally displayed in the Code window.

To display line numbers:

1 Open the **Tools** menu, and select **Options**.

2 Click on Basic in the left pane.

3 Tick **Line numbers** in the **Display** area.

Runtime error reports

There are some errors that will slip through these nets, but bring the program crashing to a halt at some point during its execution. Typically these errors revolve around data types – the data that you are attempting to pass from one variable, function or control to another is of the wrong type for its target. A second common cause is trying to use a control, a file or other object which doesn't exist. You may have misspelt the name, or changed it, or deleted the object during an earlier edit.

If you are running the program from within the Studio, the line where the error occurred will be highlighted in green in the Code window. The error will be reported in a message box, offering you the options to **Break** or **Continue**. **Continue** closes down the program, and opens the Code window at the point where you were last working. **Break** takes you into debugging mode, where you can examine the code and your variables.

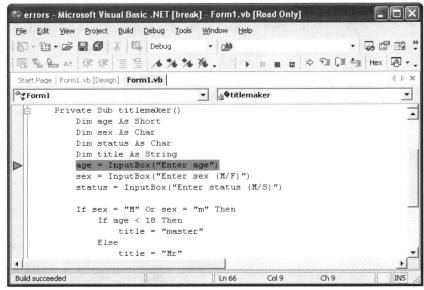

Figure 5.1

This program crashed when first run. The Break option brought us to this display. The highlighted line is the one being executed when the error occurred.

If you are running the program from its .exe file, outside the Studio, then you will get a slightly different error message box. Click the **Details** Button to get more details, make a note of them and head back to the Studio to sort out the problem.

List your variables

You will find it easier to deal with these kind of errors if you have a list of the controls and variables. A moment's reference to the list can save an hour's searching through the code. Being organised really does help!

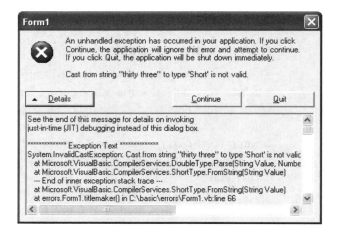

Figure 5.2

An error message from a free-standing VB program

5.2 Debugging tools

The best debugging tools are a piece of paper and a pencil. Use these to design your program, to list your variables and to dry run the design. Use them thoroughly and you won't have (m)any bugs, or much need for Visual Basic's debugging tools. These can be accessed through the Debug menu or the Debug toolbar. (Right-click on the Standard toolbar and tick **Debug** to display the toolbar.)

Figure 5.3

The Debugging tools

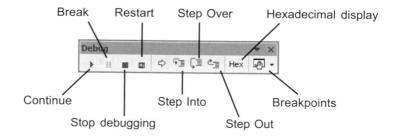

If you are getting odd results and cannot understand where they are coming from, break into the program. Use **Run > Break All**, the ⧗ Button or **[Ctrl]-[Break]** to suspend the program and go into debugging mode. A green highlight in the code will show you what was being executed when you broke in – though this will only be useful if a routine was active at that moment.

5.3 Breakpoints

Breakpoints allow you to bring a program to a halt at a predefined point in a procedure. When you set a breakpoint in a line of code and run the program, execution will halt when it reaches that line. The Breakpoints window will open, with the current line highlighted.

It is simplest to set breakpoints in the Code window while you are editing.

To set a breakpoint:

1 Right-click on the line where you want to break.

2 Select **Insert Breakpoint**.

The line will be given a red highlight and a blob placed by its side.

To remove breakpoints:

1 Click on the red blob by the line in the Code window.

Or

2 Click ⊠ in the Breakpoints window.

Any number of breakpoints may be set, and **Debug > Clear All Breakpoints** will remove them all when the bugs have been ironed out. In practice you would rarely want more than two or three at once, as too many interruptions make it difficult to

Figure 5.4

The Breakpoints window. New Breakpoints can also be set up from here.

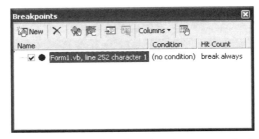

follow the flow of the program. Use breakpoints to track down one bug at a time, placing one at the last point where you know the code is good, and another further on. After running the program and checking the state of crucial variables when each breakpoint is reached, you can then bring them closer together, repeating the process until you have identified the troublesome block or line of code.

5.4 Keeping watch

A *watch* will track the values of variables, the properties of controls or the results of calculated expressions. Here is a trivial example. When I run this sums program, it keeps telling me that the answer is wrong, when it is clearly right. The relevant line reads:

```
If TextBox1.Text + TextBox2.Text = TextBox3.Text Then
    feedback.text = "Right!"
```

The simplest way to set a watch is during debugging.

1 Run the program to a breakpoint or break in at a suitable time.

2 Open the **Debug** menu, point to **Windows**, then to **Watch**, then select **Watch1**

Figure 5.5

And now I see the error of my ways!

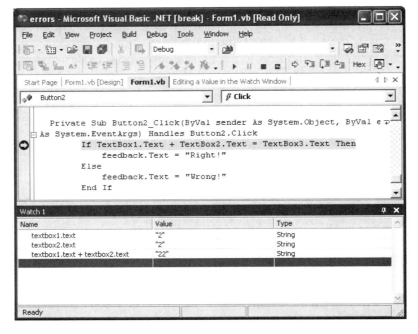

(or other ones to add further watches).

3 In the Watch window, type the name of a variable or control or type an expression in the **Name** column.

The current value in the variable or the result of the expression based on current values will be shown in the **Value** column with the data types in the **Type** column.

5.5 Stepping through

Sometimes the best way to see what is happening in a program is to slow it down to a speed at which you can follow it. For this we have the Step commands. They can be used as a way of starting execution, or restarting after a break.

◆ **Debug** > **Step Into** (or 🖼) will execute one line at a time, allowing you to use a Watch to check the progress of variables as you go.

◆ **Debug** > **Step Over** (or 🖼) will execute normally any sub or function called from within the one you are stepping through. This contrasts with **Step Into**, which would go off and work through the called routine, line by line.

◆ **Debug** > **Step Out** or the 🖼 icon will complete the current routine normally.

In stepping, the Code window opens, and the relevant line is highlighted as it is executed. As this will probably obscure the active form, be ready to switch between them as you step.

5.6 Error-trapping

On Error

The **On Error** statement can trap run-time errors. Use this to track down errors and to guard against the program crashing when users fail to behave as expected. It is particuarly valuable in filing operations, as it can trap the 'File not found', 'Drive not ready' and other common – and fatal – mistakes that can occur when accessing drives.

Errors can only be trapped within a sub or function, so if you have several places at which fatal errors are possible, each must have its own routine. The syntax takes the form:

```
Sub ....
   On Error GoTo labelled_line
   ...
Exit Sub
labelled_line:
   display error message or counteract problem
Resume label or Next
```

On Error must be early in the code, before the potential source of error. The *labelled_line* and handling-code will typically be at the end. To avoid running into this by mistake, force an early end with **Exit Sub**.

How you handle the error is entirely up to you. If the purpose of the routine is to pick up flaws in the design during debugging, then the most sensible thing to do is to display a message box telling you what the error is. This can be found from the **Err** object. Its properties include Number, Source and Description which together can identify the error very clearly.

```
On Error GoTo errmess
   ...
errmess:
   MsgBox ("The error is " & Err.Description & " Error number "
& Err.Number & " originating from " & Err.Source)
   ...
```

If the routine is there to idiot-proof the final program, then it should identify the error and either give a user-friendly message or substitute a default value, before returning to the main code. In either case, the routine must include a **Resume** statement. This tells the computer where to restart the flow of execution.

```
   Resume Next
```

This will pick up from the line following the one that produced the error. If you are using this, you should first deal with the error – perhaps by substituting a default value for the one your user failed to supply. In many cases, the error will have occurred when getting a filename or other value from the user, and the procedure will not be able to continue without a valid input. Here the best solution is to tell your user what the problem is, then Resume at a label placed past the relevant lines or at the end of the procedure. For example:

```
Private Sub AgeGroup()
   Dim age As Short
   Dim status As String
   On Error GoTo errorlines
   age = InputBox("Please enter your age")
   If (age > 16) and (age < 65) Then
      status = "Regular"
   Else
      status = "Concession"
   End If
Exit Sub
errorsub:
   MsgBox ("Invalid number given")
   Resume endline
endline:
End Sub
```

Try...Catch...Finally

This is used for trapping *exceptions* – errors thrown up by the system – and is very similar to On Error. The basic shape is:

```
Try
   code that may produce errors
```

```
Catch
   code to deal with errors
Finally
   back to main program flow
```

A simple Catch responds to all errors, but the **Catch** line can specify the type of exception, and there can be any number of them, each dealing with a different type, e.g.

```
Catch CastErr As InvalidCastException
   code to deal with invalid type casting
Catch ArgsErr As ArgumentException
   code to deal with invalid arguments
Catch
   code to deal with all other errors
```

Task 5.1

Type the last example into the **Click** procedure of a form. Run the program and click. When asked for a number, try typing in a letter and see what happens. Edit the program and turn all the error-handling lines into comments by placing a single quote at the start. Run and click again, and see what happens this time when you fail to provide a number.

6 Interacting with the system

Almost everything involves some interaction with the system. The focus here is on five particular aspects – the computer's clock, Timers, the Windows Clipboard, file handling and printing.

6.1 Date and Time

Visual Basic has a comprehensive set of functions for accessing the system clock and for handling dates and time. They are efficient and simple to use – though not without their peculiarities.

There are four properties and two functions that can interact with the clock:

Property	Returns	Example
Today	Date as numbers	03/05/04
TimeOfDay	Current time as a date value	15:14:35
Now	Date and time	03/05/04 15:14:35
Timer	Seconds since midnight	54875.465287
Function	**Returns**	**Example**
DateString	Date as formatted string	05-03-2004
TimeString	Current time as a string	"15:14:35"

These can be used to read the date and/or time. Test them by displaying the values in a message box, using lines like this:

```
MsgBox ("Today is " & Today)
```

Note that the Timer must be given with its full class definition:

```
...   Microsoft.VisualBasic.DateAndTime.Timer
```

You may find that `Today` and `TimeOfDay` are displayed in a different format from that shown here, as it depends upon the settings in the International section of the Windows Control Panel. Whatever those settings, `DateString` uses the US format "Month-Date-Year".

`Today` and `TimeOfDay` can be used to set the date and/or time. The new values must be given in Date value form enclosed in #; e.g.

```
Today = #25/12/2004#
```

This will set the date to Christmas, if you can't wait for it any longer. When setting the time, you can use a 12 or 24-hour clock, and the seconds are optional. The syntax checker will automatically convert the time value to standard form.

```
TimeOfDay = #15:05#
TimeOfDay = #03:05 PM#
TimeOfDay = #15:05:00#
```

These will all result in the follow expression when you move the cursor off the line.

```
TimeOfDay = #03:05:00 PM#
```

DateString and TimeString can also be used to set the date and/or time, but these take string values. Visual Basic can recognise dates in a number of string formats. Whether you present it with "3/5/04", "03-05-04", "3 May 2004", "3rd May 2004" or any similar combination, it will treat it as the same date.

Calculating with dates

Counting the days until the end of term? Try this,

```
Private Sub Button1_Click(ByVal sender As System.Object, ByVal e
As System.EventArgs) Handles Button1.Click
    Dim holidate As Date
    Dim myHoliday As Date
    Dim holiday As String
    Dim days As Short

    MsgBox("Today is " & Today)
    holiday = InputBox("When is your next holiday?")
    holidate = CDate(holiday)
    days = DateDiff(DateInterval.Day, Today, holidate)
    MsgBox("You have " & days & " days to wait")
    myHoliday = DateAdd(DateInterval.Day, 10, Today)
    MsgBox("I'm off in 10 days - on this date " & myHoliday)
End Sub
```

This uses three functions for manipulating dates:

- CDate(datestring) converts a date string to a date value;
- DateDiff(intervalType, Date1, Date2) calculates the difference between two dates, counting in intervalType units, e.g. this finds the number of days to my next birthday:

    ```
    DateDiff(DateInterval.Day, Today, #05/04/05#)
    ```

- DateAdd(intervalType, Number, Date) adds *Number* of *IntervalType* to the *Date* value to give a new date.

> ### Task 6.1
>
> Type the Holiday calculator into the Button_Click sub and test it with a variety of dates in different formats. How comprehensive is Visual Basic's date recognition?

6.2 Timers

From time to Timers. Code attached to a Timer control is executed regularly, at a fixed interval, no matter what is happening elsewhere. The interval can be set at the Properties window or in the code, and is given in 1/1000ths of a second. Here's a simple demo program – and you can't get much simpler than a program that only has one line of code!

1 Place a **Timer** control (⏱) on a form, along with a **Label** named *lblClock*.

2 Set the Timer's **Interval** property to 1000 and **Enabled** to *True*.

3 Give *lblClock* a chunky 'digital' font and set its **BackColor** and **BorderStyle** to make it stand out.

4 Double-click on the Timer to open its **Tick** event handler in the code window. Add this line:

```
lblClock = TimeOfDay
```

5 Build and run, and watch the clock for a while.

The Interval is measured in milliseconds – which is why 1000 gives a one-second timer – and is stored as a 32-bit integer, so can take any value up to 2 billion or so. The code on the Tick event is only executed if Enabled is True, and that can be toggled on or off at any point during the program. What this means is that you can set a Timer to run its code after any length of interval and either to do so regularly or as a one-off.

This next example shows more of the flexibility of Timers. It uses two – one makes a block appear after a random interval, the other starts counting in tenths of a second. When the user clicks on the block, the counter stops, and the process starts again. When you've got the core program running, you might like to add a few refinements, such as 'best time' and 'average time' displays – and a proper exit!

1 Place these four controls on a form (which should be at least 400 × 400):

- a **Label**, named *lblCount*, tucked away in a corner
- a **PictureBox**, named *picBlock*, 24 × 24, with a distinct **BackColor**, but with **Visible** set to *False*
- a **Timer**, *timeShow*, with **Enabled** set to *True* and an **Interval** of 1000
- a **Timer**, *timeCount*, with **Enabled** set to *False* and an **Interval** of 100

2 Add the following code to the appropriate event handlers.

```
Public Class Form1
    Inherits System.Windows.Forms.Form
    Dim count As Integer                    ' general variable for counting
Windows Form Designer generated code
    Private Sub timeShow_Tick(ByVal sender As System.Object, ByVal e As
System.EventArgs) Handles timeShow.Tick
    picBlock.Top = Int(Rnd() * 400)         ' to suit a form of 400×400
    picBlock.Left = Int(Rnd() * 400)
    picBlock.Visible = True
    timeShow.Enabled = False                ' turn off this timer
    count = 0
    timeCount.Enabled = True                ' turn on the counter
End Sub
    Private Sub timeCount_Tick(ByVal sender As System.Object, ByVal e As
System.EventArgs) Handles timeCount.Tick
    lblCount.Text = count                   ' display the count
    count += 1
End Sub
    Private Sub picBlock_Click(ByVal sender As System.Object, ByVal e As
System.EventArgs) Handles picBlock.Click
    timeCount.Enabled = False               ' turn on the counter
    timeShow.Interval = Int(Rnd() * 2000)   ' set the interval
    timeShow.Enabled = True                 ' turn on the Show timer
End Sub
End Class
```

You can use Timers to create fixed delays, to limit the time the system waits for an input from the user, or for animation. (See Chapter 8.)

The timer demo
game in action

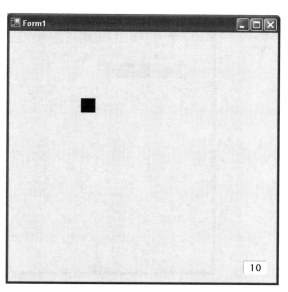

6.3   Using the Clipboard

If you – and your users – are happy working with the keyboard shortcuts
([**Ctrl**]+[**X**] to Cut, [**Ctrl**]+[**C**] to Copy, and [**Ctrl**]+[**V**] to Paste), then you can use
the standard Windows Clipboard for cutting and pasting text without writing a
single line of code. The shortcuts are there, simply because you are in Windows.

If you want to do the job properly and give your users Cut and Paste Buttons or
menu options, you can access the Clipboard directly, and use its methods and
functions in your programs. Graphics, as well as text, can be copied to and from the
Clipboard –we'll stick to text for this demonstration.

There are two crucial routines that work with the Clipboard:

- the `SetDataObject` method will copy selected data into the Clipboard;
- the `GetDataObject` function will copy it into a data variable, from which it
  can then be extracted and copied into a control.

The text is selected in the usual way – by highlighting, either with the mouse or with
[Shift] and the movement keys – and is recognised as selected by the system. With
all the heavy work done by Visual Basic, the actual code is very short.

To see how it works, set up a form containing a RichTextBox, called *TextArea*
with its **Dock** property set to *Fill*. This makes the RichTextBox fill the form – and
to continue to fill it even if the user changes the size of the window. To select *Fill*,
just click on the central block in the drop-down option display for **Dock**.

You will also need a Mainmenu with items named *EditCut*, *EditCopy*, *EditPaste*
and *FileExit*. We will add more options to the menu later as we extend this program
to produce a text editor – and extend it further in the next chapter to turn it into a
simple word processor.

Figure 6.2

The form for testing
cut and paste – this
will be developed into
a text editor

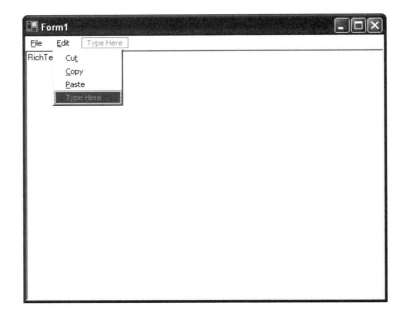

Copy

Getting data into the Clipboard is simple. RichTextBoxes have a **SelectedText** property which is the highlighted text (you will find the same property in a TextBox control). The `SetDataObject` method copies this text into the Windows Clipboard. This is all you need for the **EditCopy** sub:

```
    Private Sub EditCopy_Click(ByVal sender As Object, ByVal e
As System.EventArgs) Handles EditCopy.Click
    Clipboard.SetDataObject(TextArea.SelectedText)
End Sub
```

Cut

The **EditCut** sub is almost identical. It uses the same `SetDataObject()` method, followed by a simple line to delete the selected text.

```
    Private Sub EditCopy_Click(ByVal sender As Object, ByVal e
As System.EventArgs) Handles EditCopy.Click
    Clipboard.SetDataObject(TextArea.SelectedText)
    TextArea.SelectedText = ""
End Sub
```

Paste

Getting data out of the Clipboard is a little trickier. The problem is that any sort of data can be stored in there, so you need to check that it is suitable for copying into wherever you are going to put it.

Clipboard data is of the type `IDataObject`. If we have a variable of this type, we can copy the Clipboard contents into it and then check its nature with the `GetDataPresent()` method, from the IDataObject class. This compares the data to a given format (`DataFormats.Text` in this case) and returns *True* if it is the same.

```
Dim data As IDataObject = Clipboard.GetDataObject()
    If data.GetDataPresent(DataFormats.Text) Then …
```

To copy the text from the data object into our *TextArea*, we use the `GetData()` method – this needs to be told the format (and it is `DataFormats.Text` again).

```
    TextArea.SelectedText = data.GetData(DataFormats.Text)
```

That line will replace the selected text with the contents of the Clipboard, or if nothing is selected, it will insert the new text at the current cursor position. We can put these together to make a **EditPaste** subroutine:

```
    Private Sub EditPaste_Click(ByVal sender As Object, ByVal
e As System.EventArgs) Handles EditPaste.Click
    Dim data As IDataObject = Clipboard.GetDataObject()
    If data.GetDataPresent(DataFormats.Text) Then
        TextArea.SelectedText = data.GetData(DataFormats.Text)
    End If
End Sub
```

Task 6.2

Implement the Clipboard testing program, adding an Exit routine to the **FileExit** menu option. To prove to this uses the standard Clipboard, run the program, then cut and paste its text between it and any word-processor.

6.4 File handling dialog boxes

We met the colour dialog box in the last chapter. There are another half a dozen of these components, including dialog boxes for filing, printing, and setting fonts. We will use the **Open, Save**, **Print** and **Print Preview** dialog boxes in this chapter. All are handled in much the same way and serve similar purposes – dialog boxes are used for collecting options and information. The file-handling and printing operations must be run from elsewhere in the code.

Before we do anything else, we need to add options to the menu of our baby text editor to give us a means of accessing the code we are about to write. Add **Open, Save**, **Save As**, **Print** and **Print Preview** options to the **File** menu.

The Open dialog box

The Open dialog box will collect the filename and location from the user. But first, we need to add one to the form.

1 Select the **OpenFileDialog** control from the Toolbox – you will find it near the bottom of the set.

2 Drop it onto the form – it will go into the component tray, with a default name of *OpenFileDialog1*.

Now we need to bring it into the code. You can make the dialog box appear with this statement:

```
OpenFileDialog1.ShowDialog()
```

But that won't get you very far as it simply makes the box appear. It is more useful to embed it in the expression:

```
If OpenFileDialog1.ShowDialog() = DialogResult.OK Then…
```

This displays the dialog box, and waits until the user has selected the file and pressed **OK**.

Any of the dialog box's properties can be set before it is called, or read afterwards. In practice, all you really need is the resulting **FileName**. This is passed to the Open or Load method of the control into which the file is to be loaded. In this case, it is going into the RichTextBox called *TextArea*, and RichTextBoxes have a `LoadFile()` method. That give us the line:

```
TextArea.LoadFile(OpenFileDialog1.FileName)
```

Figure 6.3

The Open dialog box, with a Rich Text filter

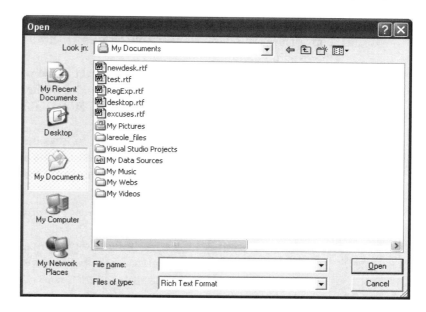

It is often useful to set the **Filter** property, which determines the file types to display. The filter has two parts: the description and the *.extension, these are written in quotes, separated by a bar, e.g. to filter for plain text files you would use:

```
OpenFileDialog1.Filter = "Text |*.txt"
```

We are using a RichTextBox, and that naturally holds data in rich text format, so the filter we need here is this:

```
OpenFileDialog1.Filter = "Rich Text Format|*.rtf"
```

You may sometimes want to start at a specific folder. If so, set the **InitialDirectory** property before calling the dialog box. It's an unnecessary complication here.

Let's put these lines together to get our file opening routine.

```
Private Sub FileOpen_Click(ByVal sender As System.Object, ByVal e As
System.EventArgs) Handles FileOpen.Click
   OpenFileDialog1.Filter = "Rich Text Format|*.rtf"
   If OpenFileDialog1.ShowDialog() = DialogResult.OK Then
      TextArea.LoadFile(OpenFileDialog1.FileName)
      myfilename = OpenFileDialog1.FileName
   End If
End Sub
```

Notice that the filename is stored in the variable *myfilename* – a String declared at the top of the code. The program will need to know what the file was called when it is time to save it again.

The Save As routine

The big difference between opening and saving files is that Windows applications normally have two routines for saving – **Save** and **Save As**. **Save As** uses the

SaveFileDialog to get the filename and/or location for saving a new file or a new copy of an existing file. **Save** simply resaves a file, with the same name, overwriting the existing copy.

The **SaveFileDialog** is used in almost the same way as the **OpenFileDialog** – which you would expect as they are two sides of the same coin. First get the box into reach of your program. Locate the **SaveFileDialog** control in the Toolbox and drop it into the component tray.

The basic code for the **Save As** routine follows the pattern of the Open routine. The **Filter** is (optionally) set beforehand to limit the display to files of the selected type, and once **OK** is clicked, the **FileName** is passed to *TextArea*'s **Save** routine. Finally, the filename is stored for later use.

```
Private Sub FileSaveAs_Click(ByVal sender As System.Object, ByVal e
As System.EventArgs) Handles FileSaveAs.Click
        SaveFileDialog1.Filter = "Rich Text Format|*.rtf"
        If SaveFileDialog1.ShowDialog() = DialogResult.OK Then
            TextArea.SaveFile(SaveFileDialog1.FileName)
            myfilename = SaveFileDialog1.FileName
        End If
    End Sub
```

The Save routine is rather simpler. The only essential code is:

```
        TextArea.SaveFile(myfilename)
```

That will save the contents of *TextArea* using the name stored in *myfilename*. However, we really should check that a name is stored there, and advise the user to run the **Save As** routine if necessary. (A most sophisticated program would automatically switch to the Save As routine for an unsaved file, but we are keeping things simple here!)

```
Private Sub FileSave_Click(ByVal sender As System.Object, ByVal e
As System.EventArgs) Handles FileSave.Click
    If myfilename = "" Then
       MsgBox("Please use File Save As")
    Else
       TextArea.SaveFile(myfilename)
    End If
End Sub
```

6.5 Printing

Printing is one of the trickier areas of computing. Taking data formatted for output to one complex machine, reformatting it and copying it out to another complex machine is inevitably going to raise difficulties. Unfortunately, Visual Basic does not make it any easier.

Printing revolves around the **Print Document** in general and its `PrintPage()` method in particular. The Print Document is where the data is assembled for output to the printer; `PrintPage()` is the method which assembles the data – and you have to write its code yourself. The example given here will handle a single page of plain text. Printing multi-page formatted documents raises problems way beyond the scope of this introductory book.

Start by placing a **PrintDocument** control on your form – it will drop into the component tray. If you double-click on it, you will be taken into its `PrintPage()` method in the Code window.

The arguments to PrintPage include e, the `PrintPageEventsArgs`, which define the object to be printed. This is a `Graphics` object, and to get text into it, we need to use the `DrawString()` method. The code will take this form:

```
e.Graphics.DrawString(TextArea.Text, myFont, myBrush, x, y)
```

The purpose of *TextArea.Text*, *myFont* and *myBrush* should be obvious. *e* refers to the PrintDocument; *x* and *y* here fix the top left corner of the printing area. You can give these as literal values, but it is better to use the margins of the page. The PrintDocument has *MarginBounds.Top* and *MarginBounds.Left* properties – these can be copied into variables for convenient handling.

```
Dim y As Single = e.MarginBounds.Top
```

Put that all together and we have a very basic PrintPage routine.

Double-click on the PrintDocument control to go into the code window – it will open at the `PrintPage` sub.

```
Private Sub PrintDocument1_PrintPage(ByVal sender As System.Object,
ByVal e As System.Drawing.Printing. PrintPageEventArgs) Handles
PrintDocument1.PrintPage
    Dim y As Single = e.MarginBounds.Top
    Dim x As Single = e.MarginBounds.Left
    Dim myFont As Font = Workspace.Font
    Dim myBrush As New SolidBrush(Color.Black)
    e.Graphics.DrawString(TextArea.Text, myFont, myBrush, x, y)
End Sub
```

If you simply want to print to the default machine, with the default settings, then all you need is to run the PrintDocument's `Print()` method:

```
PrintDocument1.Print()
```

Write that into FilePrint menu item's Click sub, and see what happens.

The Print dialog box

Drag a **PrintDialog** control from the Toolbox into the component tray before you do anything else.

Like the Open and Save dialog boxes, this collects data from the user and feeds it back into the code. Much of the feedback is invisible. The choice of printer, number of copies and the like are passed automatically between the PrintDialog and PrintDocument objects through the **PrinterSettings**. All we have to do is set up the link between these components at the start.

Our revised Print routine, using the dialog box, looks like this:

```
PrintDialog1.Document = PrintDocument1
If PrintDialog1.ShowDialog() = DialogResult.OK Then
   PrintDocument1.Print()
End If
```

Print Preview

If your print routine is working, then setting up a print preview is a piece of cake. The PrintPreviewDialog does everything for you – all you need to do is bring the control onto your form (it will go into the tray with the other dialog boxes), and write a little bit of code to link the PrintDocument to it. Here's the print preview routine in its entirety!

```
PrintPreviewDialog1.Document = PrintDocument1
PrintPreviewDialog1.ShowDialog()
```

The Page Setup dialog box

This control is unusable if your PC is set for metric units of measure as it automatically converts the margin settings into hundredths of an inch, dividing them by 2.54 when you close the box.

6.6 Exercises

6.1   Design and write a program that uses the internal clock and the `Timer` property to test reaction times. Store the time at the start of the test by the statement `starttime = Microsoft.VisualBasic.DateAndTime.Timer`. Note that the value will be a Double.

6.2   Use a Timer to produce a countdown from 10 down to 1, at one-second intervals.

6.3   Create a program that allows the user to load an image file into a PictureBox. The central line of code will read something like this:

```
PictureBox1.Image = Image.FromFile(filename)
```

Possible solutions to Exercises 6.1 and 6.2 are given in the Appendix.

7 Text processing

In this chapter, we will turn our text editor into a very basic word processor, by adding Find and Replace routines, so that text can be manipulated more efficiently, and some fonts and paragraph formatting facilities.

7.1 String manipulation

Before we can write our Find and Replace commands, we need to dip into Visual Basic's string manipulation facilities. There are two distinct sets of these: the Visual Basic run-time library has around a dozen functions, and the String class has a larger body of rather more complex methods. The two sets overlap, and where they do, the library function is usually simpler to implement, while the String method offers more advanced options.

We will be using two functions and one String method in our Find and Replace routines. Let's have a look at those, and glance at some other string manipulators while we are in the area.

The InStr( ) function

`InStr()` will look for the presence of one string within another, and return the position of the first matching character. The basic syntax is:

position = InStr(*start*, *basetext*, *searchtext*)

start is the character position at which to start checking. If this is omitted, the check starts at the beginning. As with all string functions, the first letter is at 1. This contrasts with String methods, which count letter positions from 0.

Here it is at work:

```
Dim basetext As String  = "The quick brown fox"
Dim searchtext As String = "brown"
Dim found As Short
found = InStr(1, basetext, searchtext)
```

After this, *found* will hold 11.

By moving the *start* value forward, you can look for further occurrences of the *searchtext*. For example:

```
Dim basetext As String
Dim searchtext As String
Dim found As Short
Dim start As Short = 1
basetext = "The quick brown fox jumped over the lazy dog"
searchtext = "o"
Do
    found = InStr(start, basetext, searchtext)
    MsgBox("Found at " & found)
    start = found + 1          ' continue from the next character
Loop While start < Len(basetext)
```

The messagebox will show the values 13, 18, 28 and 43.

Len()

I slipped another function into that last example! Its meaning should have been easy to guess, from its name and context.

```
Len(text)
```

returns the length of the string.

Case functions

"A" is not the same as "a", but when searching for text, you may not know – or care – the case of the characters. Switching between upper and lower case is easy. There are two functions, and they can be used on characters or on whole strings.

Lcase()

```
LCase(char)    or    LCase(string)
```

These change the character or string to lower case, e.g.

```
lowerchar = Lcase("A")
```

lowerchar now holds "a".

```
lowertext = Lcase("AbCdEfGhIjKlM")
```

lowertext now holds "abcdefghijklm".

Ucase()

The equivalent upper case functions are:

```
UCase(char)    or    LCase(string)
```

We can combine these with InStr() to produce a case-insensitive search routine:

```
found = InStr(start, LCase(basetext), LCase(searchtext))
```

UCase would work just as well – but don't use one of each!

7.2 String slicing

These three functions will *copy* a chunk from one string into another – the base string is not changed.

```
newstring = Mid(basestring, startchar, number)
```

`Mid()` is a simple function. It copies *number* characters from *startchar* of *oldstring* into *newstring*. If number is omitted, it copies to the end of the string.

```
newstring = Microsoft.VisualBasic.Left(oldstring, number)
```

This copies *number* characters from the left (start) of *oldstring* into *newstring*. As `Left` could be mistaken for a property of a control, you have to specify Microsoft.VisualBasic when using `Left()` function. `Mid()` is also part of the same library, but you do not need to specify the namespace when using it.

```
newstring = Mid(oldstring, 1, number)
```

does the same job as `Left()` and is quicker to write!

```
newstring = Microsoft.VisualBasic.Right(oldstring, number)
```

This likewise copies *number* characters from the right-hand end of *oldstring* into *newstring*. And once again, we have a `Mid()` alternative, though it's not that much simpler this time:

```
newstring = Mid(oldstring, length-number, number)
```

A Proper( ) function

We now have enough to create a useful `Proper()` function – one that makes sure proper names (of people, places, etc.) have their first character in upper case and the rest in lower case.

First, the one-step-at-a-time version. This uses two local variables to hold the initial letter and the rest of the name – both sliced out of the incoming string by variations on `Mid()`. They are each forced into the appropriate case, then the two are joined together to feed back into the properly-formed string.

```
Private Function proper(ByVal incoming As String) As String
   Dim initial As String
   Dim rest As String
   initial = Mid(incoming, 1, 1)
   initial = UCase(initial)
   rest = Mid(incoming, 2)
   rest = LCase(rest)
   proper = initial & rest
End Function
```

And here's the compact version. This time `LCase()` and `UCase()` are wrapped around the `Mid()` expressions, and fed to the proper name without going through temporary variables.

```
Private Function proper(ByVal incoming As String) As String
   proper = UCase(Mid(incoming, 1, 1)) & LCase(Mid(incoming, 2))
End Function
```

The Mid( ) statement

There is also a `Mid()` statement which copies text *into* a string, replacing the existing characters.

```
Mid(oldstring, startchar, number) = newstring
```

For example:

```
Dim oldstring As String
oldstring = "The quick brown fox"
Mid(oldstring, 11, 5) ="black"
MsgBox(oldstring)
Mid(oldstring, 11, 3) = "red"
MsgBox(oldstring)
```

The first MsgBox will display "The quick black fox", the second one will display "The quick redck fox". Which points up one of the limitations of this statement – you can only really use it to replace a string with another of the same length. There is a better way of replacing text.

The Replace( ) method

This is a member of the **String** class. It will replace one piece of text with another – of any length – inside a string. The syntax is:

```
newstring = oldstring.Replace(oldtext, newtext)
```

Here's that last example, but with `Replace()` instead of `Mid()`.

```
Dim oldstring As String
Dim newstring As String
oldstring = "The quick brown fox"
newstring = oldstring.Replace("brown", "black")
MsgBox(newstring)
newstring = oldstring.Replace("black", "red")
MsgBox(newstring)
```

This time the MsgBoxes read "The quick black fox" – as before, and "The quick red fox" – with "red" neatly replacing the longer "black".

Other String members

Two other String class members that you might find useful are the `IndexOf()` method and the `Length` property.

   `IndexOf()` is equivalent to the `InStr()` function, returning the start position of one string within another. The syntax is:

```
place = basetext.IndexOf(searchtext)
```

Always remember that String methods start counting from 0, unlike string functions, where the first character is at 1. For example:

```
Dim basetext As String
Dim searchtext As String
Dim found As Short
basetext = "The quick brown fox"
searchtext = "brown"
found = basetext.IndexOf(searchtext)
```

This will give *found* a value of 10.

The Length property

`Length` produces the same results as the `Len()` function.

```
textLength = basetext.Length
```

If *basetext* held "The quick brown fox", *textLength* would have a value of 19.

> **Task 7.1**
>
> Look up String class members in the Help system to find out more about this set of methods and properties. Select at least one method and one property – other than those we have used so far – and write code to demonstrate them.

7.3 Find and Replace

Let's put these functions and methods to work and develop Find and Replace routines for our word processor.

Find

This revolves around `InStr()`, which searches the text for the given string, and that part of the routine should need little further explanation.

```
firstChar = InStr(startAt, text, target)
```

This gives us the position of the first character of the matching string, or 0 if there is no match.

The more interesting code is that which deals with the text after it has been found. If there is only a single instance of the found text, we can highlight it by making it the **SelectedText** of *TextArea*. To do this, we need to know where the selection starts and how long it is. The start position is at 1 less than where the match was found (because string functions count from 1, but String members count from 0).

```
TextArea.SelectionStart = firstChar - 1
```

The length is simply the length of the target string:

```
TextArea.SelectionLength = target.Length
```

Setting those two properties defines the **SelectedText**, and it will be shown highlighted when the routine ends.

If we want to be able to find all the occurrences of the matching text, then we need to add two more things to the routine. The first is a loop to keep working through the text. That is straightforward, though you must remember to move the start position on each time round:

```
startAt = firstChar + 1
```

Highlighting the matches is trickier, as the SelectedText can only be a single area, and also the normal SelectedText highlight does not show up while the routine is working through the loop. The solution offered here is to recolour the text red – the current colour is recorded beforehand, so that it can be restored later.

```
oldcol = Workspace.SelectionColor
TextArea.SelectionColor = Color.Red
   . . .
TextArea.SelectionColor = oldcol
```

The full routine follows – but first you need somewhere to place it. Add a **Find** item to the **Edit** menu, naming it *EditFind*. You might as well add the **Replace** item (named *EditReplace*) while you are at it.

```
Private Sub EditFind_Click(ByVal sender As System.Object, ByVal e
As System.EventArgs) Handles EditFind.Click
  Dim target, text As String
  Dim firstChar As Short = 0
  Dim startAt As Short = 1
  Dim findNext As Short
  Dim oldcol As Object
  target = InputBox("Text to find", "Find")
  If target = Nothing Then Exit Sub
  text = TextArea.Text
  Do
     firstChar = InStr(startAt, text, target)
     If firstChar = 0 Then
       MsgBox("Not found")
       Exit Do
     Else
        TextArea.SelectionStart = firstChar - 1
        TextArea.SelectionLength = target.Length
        oldcol = TextArea.SelectionColor
        TextArea.SelectionColor = Color.Red
     End If
     findNext = MsgBox("Find next?", MsgBoxStyle.YesNo, "Find")
     TextArea.SelectionColor = oldcol
     startAt = firstChar + 1
  Loop Until findNext <> 6
End Sub
```

Replace

All that is really essential here is to collect the text to find and to replace, then apply the `Replace()` method – and as this automatically replaces *every* matching occurrence, we don't even need to worry about running it through a loop. This would do the job:

```
Dim target, text As String
target = InputBox("Text to find", "Find and Replace")
newtext = InputBox("Text to replace it with", "Find and Replace")
TextArea.Text = TextArea.Text.Replace(target, text )
```

The routine given here is more complicated than that because I've added some checks. It uses `InStr()`, first to see if the *target* text is there, and then to locate every occurrence of it – these are then recoloured, as in the Find routine. The code then asks for confirmation before doing the replacement.

As it stands, if the user decides not to replace the found strings, this routine leaves them coloured red. You may want to add a further block to run through the text again, and turn them back to the original text colour.

```
Private Sub EditReplace_Click(ByVal sender As System.Object, ByVal e
As System.EventArgs) Handles EditReplace.Click
   Dim target, text As String
   Dim newtext As String
   Dim editedtext As String
   Dim firstChar As Short = 0
   Dim startAt As Short = 1
   Dim numChars As Short
   Dim confirm As Short
   target = InputBox("Text to find", "Find and Replace")
   If target = Nothing Then Exit Sub
   numChars = target.Length
   newtext = InputBox("Text to replace it with", "Find and Replace")
   text = TextArea.Text
   firstChar = InStr(startAt, text, target)
   If firstChar = 0 Then
      MsgBox("Not found")
   Else
' recolour all occurrences of the matching text
      Do
         TextArea.SelectionStart = firstChar - 1
         TextArea.SelectionLength = target.Length
         TextArea.SelectionColor = Color.Red
         startAt = firstChar + 1
         firstChar = InStr(startAt, text, target)
      Loop Until firstChar = 0
      confirm = MsgBox("Replace all?", MsgBoxStyle.YesNo, "Replace")
      If confirm = 6 Then
```

```
            TextArea.Text  = text.Replace(target,newtext)
        End If
    End If
End Sub
```

Formatting tools

Before we add the formatting routines, we should get the menu items in place so that we can test them. The new Format menu is shown here. This has a Font Style submenu, with Bold, Italic and Underline options.

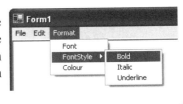

7.4 Font formatting

The Font dialog box

The Font dialog box makes font formatting ridiculously easy to implement. All you have to do is call up the box and copy the font specification from its Font property into the RichTextBox's **Font** property.

Place a **FontDialog** control in the component tray, along with the other dialog boxes, and add the following three lines of code into the menu item's `Click` sub.

```
Private Sub FormatFont_Click(ByVal sender As System.Object, ByVal e
As System.EventArgs) Handles FormatFont.Click
    If FontDialog1.ShowDialog() = DialogResult.OK Then
        TextArea.SelectionFont = FontDialog1.Font
    End If
End Sub
```

Trying to control individual elements of the font, such as turning bold on or off, is considerably more complex, as you will see shortly. Let's get the rest of the easy stuff out of the way first.

Figure 8.1

The standard Font dialog box can be called up from within Visual Basic

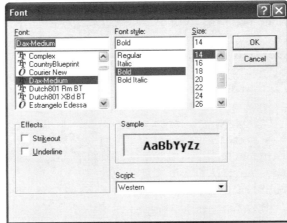

The Color dialog box

This is the standard Windows Color dialog box. It is used here to colour the font, and you'll meet it again in Chapter 8, when we look at graphics. Whatever is being coloured, the dialog box is used in the same way.

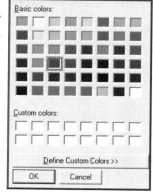

All we need to do is place the ColorDialog control in the component tray, then add a little code to copy the chosen colour over to the **SelectionColor** property – this sets the colour of the selected text.

The Color dialog box as it first appears

Here is the code to set colour:

```
    Private Sub FormatCol_Click(ByVal sender As System.Object, ByVal e
As System.EventArgs) Handles FormatCol.Click
    If ColorDialog1.ShowDialog() = DialogResult.OK Then
        TextArea.SelectionColor = ColorDialog1.Color
    End If
End Sub
```

7.5 Font.Style formatting

You can set the font style options from within the Font dialog box, but we should also offer Bold, Italic and Underline on/off switches – as most word processors do. This will take a little more work because the Bold, Italic and Underline switches are all stored in the FontStyle property. This is a single byte, and the on/off state of the switches is held in individual bits within it. You are going to have to use the bitwise operators to turn them on and off.

Logical (bitwise) operators

The operators And, Or and Xor are mainly used for combining expressions in logical tests as we saw in Chapter 3, but they can also be used for manipulating numbers at a binary level.

Here's a crash course for readers who are new to binary numbers.

Binary numbers

In any number, the value that a digit represents depends upon two things – the digit itself, and its place in the number. This is true in any system. Look at a number in our normal (base 10) system. Take the digits of 1066, right to left:

6	=	6 * 1	=	6
6	=	6 * 10	=	60
0	=	0 * 100	=	0
1	=	1 * 1000	=	1000

Each time you move a place to the left, the value of the digit increases by a factor of 10. In binary (base 2) numbers, the place value increases by 2. So, in the number 10101, the digits are worth (in base 10):

```
1   =   1 * 1    =   1
0   =   0 * 2    =   0
1   =   1 * 4    =   4
0   =   0 * 8    =   0
1   =   1 * 16   =   16
```

The standard unit of computing is the byte, which has 8 bits (binary digits) and can represent any value between 0 and 255.

128	64	32	16	8	4	2	1
0	0	0	1	0	1	0	1

You can look at binary numbers in two ways. You can combine the bits to give the overall value – 21 in the last example; but you can also use the individual bits to signify on (1) or off (0) status. The **Font.Style** property controls bold, italics, underline and strikethrough. They can be accessed individually, e.g.:

```
FontStyle.Bold
```

turns Bold on (and everything else off).

```
FontStyle.Italics
```

turns Italics on (and everything else off).

But in this context, **Bold**, **Italics** and the rest are constants, where **Bold** = 1, **Italics** = 2, **Underline** = 4 and **Strikethrough** = 8. You must have seen where this was leading – **Font.Style** is held in a single byte, and the status of the four styles are held in its last 4 bits. You can produce composite styles by turning on several bits, e.g. this turns on Bold and Underline (1 + 4 = 5).

```
FontStyle.5
```

You can also check and change the status of individual bits – and that is where And, Or and Xor come into play.

And

If you combine two numbers with And, the bits are compared and if the same bit is 1 in both numbers, then that bit in the result is 1. Looking at it in binary:

```
1 And 1 = 1
1 And 0 = 0
```

It takes a little longer to demonstrate in base 10.

```
89 And 69 =
```

Convert to binary:

	128	64	32	16	8	4	2	1	
89 =	0	1	0	1	1	0	0	1	
69 =	0	1	0	0	0	1	0	1	
	0	1	0	0	0	0	0	1	= 65

We can use this to test the status of bits. Looking back to the FontStyle values, if you had a variable *myStyle* which held the style setting, the expression:

```
If (myStyle And 2) = 2 Then...
```

will give a *True* result if the Italics bit is on.

Or

If you combine two numbers with Or, if either or both of the bits at one place are 1, then that bit in the result is 1.

```
1 Or 0 = 1
1 Or 0 = 1
0 Or 0 = 0
```

For example,

```
89 Or 69 =
```

Convert to binary:

	128	64	32	16	8	4	2	1	
89 =	0	1	0	1	1	0	0	1	
69 =	0	1	0	0	0	1	0	1	
	0	1	0	1	1	1	0	1	= 93

We can use **Or** to make sure that bits are set. Sticking with the FontStyle example, this expression:

```
myStyle = (myStyle Or 1)
```

will turn on Bold if it is not already on, or leave it on if it is.

Xor

This is the eXclusive Or. This only gives a 1 result if one or other – but not both – of the compared bits is 1.

```
1 Xor 0 = 1
1 Xor 1 = 0
0 Xor 0 = 0
```

For example,

```
89 Xor 69 =
```

Convert to binary:

	128	64	32	16	8	4	2	1	
89 =	0	1	0	1	1	0	0	1	
69 =	0	1	0	0	0	1	0	1	
	0	0	0	1	1	1	0	0	= 28

We can use Xor to 'flip' bits – toggling them between 1 and 0. This will turn Bold on if it is off, or off if it is on:

```
myStyle = (myStyle Xor 1)
```

Setting Font.Style with Xor

We noted earlier that the **Font.Style** property has four components:

Bold	=	1 (when on)
Italics	=	2 (when on)
Underline	=	4 (when on)
Strikethrough	=	8 (when on) – not implemented here

There are predefined constants with these values, which you can use to set single options, e.g. **FontStyle.Bold** has a value of 1. If we Xor these against the existing style, it will toggle the options on or off. Suppose Bold and Italics are currently on. Style will have a value of 3. The expression:

```
TextArea.SelectionFont.Style Xor FontStyle.Bold
```

will result in a value of 2 – toggling Bold off. Look at the bits:

							U	I	B	
Font.Style	0	0	0	0	0	0	1	1	= Italic on, Bold on
FontStyle.Bold	0	0	0	0	0	0	0	1	
new Style	0	0	0	0	0	0	1	0	= Italic on, Bold off

Do it again, and the result will be 3 as Bold is toggled back on. That gives us this routine for Bold – the Italic and Underline versions are basically the same:

```
Private Sub FontStyleBold_Click(ByVal sender As System.Object, ByVal
e As System.EventArgs) Handles FontStyleBold.Click
  newStyle = TextArea.SelectionFont.Style Xor FontStyle.Bold
  setfont()         'see below
End Sub
```

We are not actually setting the font options here. To redefine the font, we have to create a new **Font** object, with the changed options, and copy that to the text's font. The Font object has three arguments:

```
    Font (Family, Size, Style)
```

Family is the font name (you can also use a generic name, e.g. "Sans", instead of specifying an exact font). You could define a new font like this:

```
    headerFont = New Font ("Arial", 15, FontStyle.Bold)
```

We only want to set the style, but you must give all three arguments. The solution is to pick up the current FontFamily and Size settings from the SelectionFont property, and reuse them when we define the new font.

```
Private Sub setfont()
  Dim MyFont As System.Drawing.Font
  MyFont = TextArea.SelectionFont               'current settings
  TextArea.SelectionFont = New Font(MyFont.FontFamily, MyFont.Size,
newStyle)
End Sub
```

7.6 Worked example: a simple word processor

Here is the complete code for our simple word processor. If you started from the basis of the text editor from Chapter 6 and have added the routines that we have developed in the last dozen pages, then you should have most of it already – though not necessarily in the same order.

```
Public Class Form1
    Inherits  System.Windows.Forms.Form
    Dim myfilename As String
    Dim newStyle As System.Drawing.FontStyle

Windows Form Designer generated code

    Private Sub FileExit_Click(ByVal sender As System.Object, ByVal e As
System.EventArgs) Handles FileExit.Click
        End
End Sub

    Private Sub FileOpen_Click(ByVal sender As System.Object, ByVal e As
System.EventArgs) Handles FileOpen.Click
        OpenFileDialog1.Filter = "Rich Text Format|*.rtf"
        If OpenFileDialog1.ShowDialog() = DialogResult.OK Then
            TextArea.LoadFile(OpenFileDialog1.FileName)
            myfilename = OpenFileDialog1.FileName
        End If
End Sub

    Private Sub FileSave_Click(ByVal sender As System.Object, ByVal e As
System.EventArgs) Handles FileSave.Click
        If myfilename = "" Then
            MsgBox("Please use File Save As")
        Else
            TextArea.SaveFile(myfilename)
        End If
End Sub

    Private Sub FileSaveAs_Click(ByVal sender As System.Object, ByVal e
As System.EventArgs) Handles FileSaveAs.Click
        SaveFileDialog1.Filter = "Rich Text Format|*.rtf"
        If SaveFileDialog1.ShowDialog() = DialogResult.OK Then
            TextArea.SaveFile(SaveFileDialog1.FileName)
            myfilename = SaveFileDialog1.FileName
        End If
End Sub

    Private Sub PrintDocument1_PrintPage(ByVal sender As System.Object,
ByVal e As System.Drawing.Printing.PrintPageEventArgs) Handles
PrintDocument1.PrintPage
```

```vbnet
    Dim y As Single = e.MarginBounds.Top
    Dim x As Single = e.MarginBounds.Left
    Dim printFont As New Font("Arial", 14)
    Dim myBrush As New SolidBrush(Color.Black)
    e.Graphics.DrawString(TextArea.Text, New Font("Arial", 16), myBrush, x, y)
End Sub

    Private Sub FilePrint_Click(ByVal sender As System.Object, ByVal e _
As System.EventArgs) Handles FilePrint.Click
    PrintDialog1.Document = PrintDocument1
    If PrintDialog1.ShowDialog() = DialogResult.OK Then
      PrintDocument1.Print()
    End If
End Sub

    Private Sub EditCopy_Click(ByVal sender As Object, ByVal e As _
System.EventArgs) Handles EditCopy.Click
    Clipboard.SetDataObject(TextArea.SelectedText)
End Sub

    Private Sub EditCut_Click(ByVal sender As Object, ByVal e As _
System.EventArgs) Handles EditCut.Click
    Clipboard.SetDataObject(TextArea.SelectedText)
    TextArea.SelectedText = ""
End Sub

    Private Sub EditPaste_Click(ByVal sender As Object, ByVal e As _
System.EventArgs) Handles EditPaste.Click
    Dim data As IDataObject = Clipboard.GetDataObject()
    If data.GetDataPresent(DataFormats.Text) Then
      TextArea.SelectedText = data.GetData(DataFormats.Text)
    End If
End Sub

    Private Sub EditFind_Click(ByVal sender As System.Object, ByVal e As _
System.EventArgs) Handles EditFind.Click
    Dim target, text As String
    Dim firstChar As Short = 0
    Dim startAt As Short = 1
    Dim findNext As Short
    Dim oldcol As Object
    target = InputBox("Text to find", "Find")
    If target = Nothing Then Exit Sub
    text = TextArea.Text
    Do
      firstChar = InStr(startAt, text, target)
      If firstChar = 0 Then
        MsgBox("Not found")
```

```
          Exit Do
        Else
          TextArea.SelectionStart = firstChar - 1
          TextArea.SelectionLength = target.Length
          oldcol = TextArea.SelectionColor
          TextArea.SelectionColor = Color.Red
        End If
        findNext = MsgBox("Find the next?", MsgBoxStyle.YesNo, "Find")
        TextArea.SelectionColor = oldcol
        startAt = firstChar + 1
    Loop Until findNext <> 6
End Sub

    Private Sub EditReplace_Click(ByVal sender As System.Object, ByVal
e As System.EventArgs) Handles EditReplace.Click
    Dim target, text As String
    Dim newtext As String
    Dim editedtext As String
    Dim firstChar As Short = 0
    Dim startAt As Short = 1
    Dim numChars As Short
    Dim confirm As Short

    target = InputBox("Text to find", "Find and Replace")
    If target = Nothing Then Exit Sub
    numChars = target.Length
    newtext = InputBox("Text to replace it with", "Find and Replace")
    text = TextArea.Text
    firstChar = InStr(startAt, text, target)
    If firstChar = 0 Then
      MsgBox("Not found")
    Else
      Do
        TextArea.SelectionStart = firstChar - 1
        TextArea.SelectionLength = target.Length
        TextArea.SelectionColor = Color.Red
        startAt = firstChar + 1
        firstChar = InStr(startAt, text, target)
      Loop Until firstChar = 0
      confirm = MsgBox("Replace all?", MsgBoxStyle.YesNo, "Replace")
      If confirm = 6 Then TextArea.Text = text.Replace(target,
newtext)
    End If
End Sub

    Private Sub FormatFont_Click(ByVal sender As System.Object, ByVal
e As System.EventArgs) Handles FormatFont.Click
```

```
      If FontDialog1.ShowDialog() = DialogResult.OK Then
         TextArea.SelectionFont = FontDialog1.Font
      End If
   End Sub

   Private Sub setfont()
   Dim MyFont As System.Drawing.Font = TextArea.SelectionFont
   TextArea.SelectionFont = New Font(MyFont.FontFamily, MyFont.Size,
newStyle)
   End Sub

   Private Sub FontStyleBold_Click(ByVal sender As System.Object,
ByVal e As System.EventArgs) Handles FontStyleBold.Click
      newStyle = TextArea.SelectionFont.Style Xor FontStyle.Bold
      setfont()
   End Sub

   Private Sub FontStyleItalic_Click(ByVal sender As System.Object,
ByVal e As System.EventArgs) Handles FontStyleItalic.Click
      newStyle = TextArea.SelectionFont.Style Xor FontStyle.Italic
      setfont()
   End Sub

   Private Sub FontStyleUnderline_Click(ByVal sender As
System.Object, ByVal e As System.EventArgs) Handles
FontStyleUnderline.Click
      newStyle = TextArea.SelectionFont.Style Xor FontStyle.Underline
      setfont()
   End Sub

   Private Sub FormatCol_Click(ByVal sender As System.Object, ByVal e
As System.EventArgs) Handles FormatCol.Click
      If ColorDialog1.ShowDialog() = DialogResult.OK Then
         TextArea.SelectionColor = ColorDialog1.Color
      End If
   End Sub

End Class
```

Tidying up code

The order in which subs appear in the code of a program make not the slightest difference to the Visual Basic system. However, if you are likely to be coming back to a program after some time, or if other people may need to work on it, then setting the subs in some kind of logical order will make it more readable. Use cut and paste to move whole subs – taking care to get the full header and end sub lines. You must, of course, double-check the program afterwards to make sure that it still works!

7.7 Exercises

7.1 Find out about drag and drop editing and implement it in the text editor. (The Help system is very good on this topic.)

7.2 A palindrome is a word or phrase that reads the same left to right and right to left, e.g. "rats live on no evil star" or 'Madam I'm Adam". (Note that case, spaces and punctuation are ignored.) Create a function that will return True if a string is a palindrome.

7.3 Let's code some coding. Proper cryptography is complex, so we'll make do with letter-shifting – moving the characters a set number of places up the ASCII code, so 'Basic' would become 'Fewmg' if 4 was the code number. Write routines encode and decode text in the text editor.

Possible solutions to Exercises 7.2 and 7.3 are given in the Appendix.

8 Graphics

Visual Basic offers simple ways to import and display graphic files, and you can enhance the appearance of controls, so there is limited need for drawn graphics. But there are drawing facilities, and they are worth exploring.

8.1 Basic concepts

To draw any kind of graphic in Visual Basic, you have to work through three stages:
1 Create an object on which to draw.
2 Draw the image using the methods for drawing lines, circles, rectangles, etc.
3 Display the object, with its image.

Most of the code uses properties and methods from the `System.Drawing` namespace, and in particular the `Graphics`, `Color`, `Brush` and `Pen` classes. If you put this line at the very top of your program – above `Public Class Form1`...

```
Imports System.Drawing
```

... then you won't have to type `System.Drawing` every time that you use a method or property from the namespace.

Let's have a look at the stages in more detail.

The graphics object

This defines the variable *canvas* as a graphics object – note that `System.Drawing` is essential here, even if you have imported it:

```
Dim canvas as System.Drawing.Graphics
```

This must then be associated with a form or a suitable control such as a PictureBox, to give somewhere on which to draw. Visual Basic refers to the current form as `Me`.

```
canvas = Me.CreateGraphics()
```

The two lines can be run together:

```
Dim canvas as System.Drawing.Graphics = Me.CreateGraphics()
```

The graphics area has its origin (0, 0) at the top left corner of the form, and all coordinates are given in pixels.

DrawLine()

The simplest of the drawing methods is `DrawLine()`, which draws a straight line. The syntax is:

GraphicsArea.`DrawLine`(*pen, x1, y1, x2, y2*)

GraphicsArea is the graphics object on which you want to draw.

$x1, y1, x2, y2$ simply define the start and end points of the line. The coordinates are given in pixels, counting from the top left.

The *pen* is a rather more complex concept – it is an object which sets the colour and width of the line. You can use the `Pens` class to define the pen directly in the arguments, but this only sets the colour – the width will always be 1 pixel.

```
canvas.DrawLine(Pens.Coral, 50, 50, 150, 200)
```

This draws a thin pale blue line from 50, 50 to 150, 200.

You have more control over the pen if you define it beforehand. Use the `New` constructor to create a new object, setting the colour and width. The pen can then be used in the `DrawLine()`.

```
Dim myPen As New Pen(Color.Red,5)
canvas.DrawLine(myPen, 0, 0, 250, 200)
```

This produces a 5-pixel thick red line from 0, 0 to 250, 200.

Painting the screen

The Drawing methods define the shape on the graphics area, but these alone do not make the image appear on the screen. To make it visible we have to do the drawing in, or call the drawing sub from, the `OnPaint()` base method – you will find it it the `Overrides` group in the Class list in the Code window. `OnPaint()` is called whenever the screen needs 'repainting'.

Put it all together, and we have this code (see Figure 8.1 for the display).

```
Protected Overrides Sub OnPaint(ByVal e As System.Windows.Forms.
PaintEventArgs)
   Dim canvas As System.Drawing.Graphics
   canvas = Me.CreateGraphics()
   Dim mypen As New Pen(Color.Black, 4)
   canvas.DrawLine(mypen, 0, 0, 200, 200)
   mypen.Color = Color.Red
   canvas.DrawLine(mypen, 50, 250, 400, 250)
End Sub
```

In practice, you will get a neater and easier to read program if you write the drawing code inside subroutines, and call those from `OnPaint()`.

```
Protected Overrides Sub OnPaint(ByVal e As PaintEventArgs)
   myDrawingCode()
End Sub
```

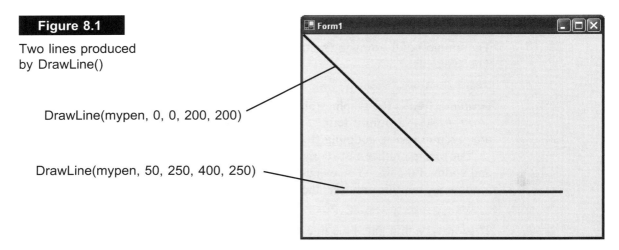

Figure 8.1

Two lines produced
by DrawLine()

DrawLine(mypen, 0, 0, 200, 200)

DrawLine(mypen, 50, 250, 400, 250)

8.2 Line drawing methods

DrawRectangle()

The syntax is almost the same as DrawLine().

GraphicsArea.DrawRectangle(*pen, x, y, width, height*)

x, y, width, height define the top left corner and the size of the rectangle. Try this – you should see a black square, 50 × 50 pixels, with its top left at 50, 50 and a red rectangle, 300 × 20 pixels, starting at 0, 150.

```
Protected Overrides Sub OnPaint(ByVal e As System.Windows.Forms.
PaintEventArgs)
   Dim canvas As System.Drawing.Graphics
   canvas = Me.CreateGraphics()
   Dim mypen As New Pen(Color.Black, 4)
   canvas.DrawRectangle(mypen, 50, 50, 50, 50)
   mypen.Color = Color.Red
   canvas.DrawRectangle(mypen, 0, 150, 300, 20)
End Sub
```

Figure 8.2

Two rectangles produced
by DrawRectangle()

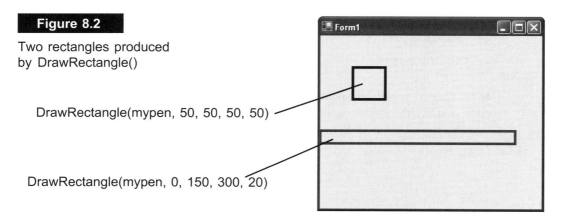

DrawRectangle(mypen, 50, 50, 50, 50)

DrawRectangle(mypen, 0, 150, 300, 20)

DrawEllipse( )

The syntax is the same as `DrawRectangle()`, with the single difference being that here the *width*, *height* define the top left corner and the size of the rectangle in which the ellipse is to be drawn.

GraphicsArea.DrawEllipse(*pen*, *x*, *y*, *width*, *height*)

If *width* and *height* are the same, of course, you will get a circle. This next example produces a small circle and a larger flattened ellipse.

```
Protected Overrides Sub OnPaint(ByVal e As System.Windows.Forms.
PaintEventArgs)
    Dim canvas As System.Drawing.Graphics
    canvas = Me.CreateGraphics()
    Dim mypen As New Pen(Color.Black, 4)
    canvas.DrawEllipse(mypen, 50, 50, 50, 50)
    mypen.Color = Color.Red
    canvas.DrawEllipse(mypen, 25, 150, 300, 100)
End Sub
```

DrawEllipse() in action

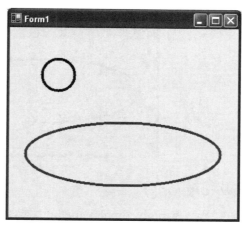

DrawArc( )

An arc is a segment of an ellipse, so it's not surprising that the `DrawArc()` method is an extended version of `DrawEllipse()`. The syntax is:

GraphicsArea.DrawEllipse(*pen*, *x*, *y*, *width*, *height*, *start*, *sweep*)

x, *y*, *width*, *height* define the bounding rectangle for the whole ellipse.
start is the angle at which the arc begins.
sweep is the angle of the arc.

In DrawArc, angles are measured in degrees, counting clockwise and starting from 3 o'clock

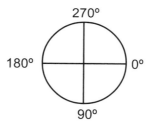

In the demo code for this, I have accompanied each `DrawArc()` command with a `DrawEllipse()` set to show the complete ellipse for the arc.

```
Protected Overrides Sub OnPaint(ByVal e As System.Windows.Forms.
PaintEventArgs)
    Dim canvas As System.Drawing.Graphics
    canvas = Me.CreateGraphics()
    Dim mypen As New Pen(Color.Black, 4)
    Dim thinpen As New Pen(Color.Gray, 1)
    canvas.DrawEllipse(thinpen, 50, 0, 100, 100)
    canvas.DrawArc(mypen, 50, 0, 100, 100, 0, 135)
    canvas.DrawEllipse(thinpen, 25, 150, 300, 100)
    canvas.DrawArc(mypen, 25, 150, 300, 100, 90, 240)
End Sub
```

Figure 8.5

Two arcs with their matching ellipses

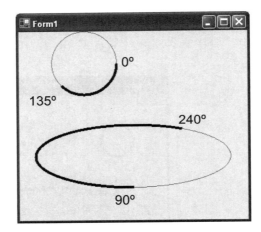

DrawPolygon( )

This is a rather more complex method. A polygon is defined by the position of its vertices, and these are given in *points* and held in an array. Both need some explanation.

In Visual Basic, a point is a data structure, consisting of a pair of x, y values. To set up a point, use the `New` constructor, giving the coordinates, e.g.

```
Dim p1 = New Point(100, 50)
```

p1 now refers to the location 100, 50.

Having created the individual points for the polygon, you then have to collect them into an array. The best way to do this is to copy the points at the time of setting up the array. The line should look something like this – note that the values for the array are enclosed in curly brackets:

```
Dim PolyPoint As Point() = {p1, p2, p3, p4, p5, p6}
```

This array is then passed to `DrawPolygon()` as an argument, e.g.

```
canvas.DrawPolygon(myPen, PolyPoint)
```

This subroutine will draw a hexagonal polygon, with sides of 125 pixels. It should be called from the `OnPaint()` subroutine.

```
Protected Overrides Sub OnPaint(ByVal e As System.Windows.Forms.
PaintEventArgs)
    Static Dim canvas As System.Drawing.Graphics
    Dim mypen As New Pen(Color.Black, 2)
    Dim mybrush As New SolidBrush(Color.Blue)
    canvas = Me.CreateGraphics()
    Dim pt1 As New Point(150, 50)
    Dim pt2 As New Point(250, 100)
    Dim pt3 As New Point(250, 225)
    Dim pt4 As New Point(150, 275)
    Dim pt5 As New Point(50, 225)
    Dim pt6 As New Point(50, 100)
    Dim curvePoints As Point() = {pt1, pt2, pt3, pt4, pt5, pt6}
    canvas.DrawPolygon(mypen, curvePoints)
End Sub
```

Figure 8.6

A hexagon drawn using
DrawPolygon()

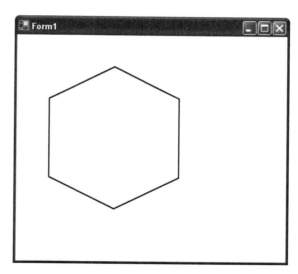

You might like to know that you can calculate the vertices of any regular polygon using the following formulae.

```
x = Int(xcentre + Sin(vertex * 2 * PI / sides) * size)
y = Int(ycentre + Cos(vertex * 2 * PI / sides) * size)
```

Where *xcentre* and *ycentre* are the coordinates of the centre of the polygon; *vertex* is the position number of the vertex, counting anticlockwise from 0; *sides* is how many sides there are; and *size* is the length of a side.

e.g. these find the coordinates of the third point of a 5-sided polygon, centred at 100, 100 with sides of 50 pixels:

```
x = Int(100 + Sin(3* 2 * PI / 5) * 50)
y = Int(100 + Cos(3* 2 * PI / 5) * 50)
```

8.3 Filled shapes

To create filled shapes, you can use the methods `FillRectangle()`, `FillEllipse()`, `FillPie()` – which produces filled arcs – and `FillPolygon()`. These are almost identical to their `Draw...` equivalents, and the shapes themselves are defined in exactly the same way. The only real difference is that you use a *pen* to draw a shape, but a *brush* to fill it with colour.

Brushes

There are several types of brushes, from the simplest, which fill a shape with a flat colour, through to gradient colourings and textured fill.

To set up a solid brush, you just supply the colour in the `New` constructor.

```
Dim myBrushS As New SolidBrush(Color.Red)
```

This shows three of the Fill methods at work. I have accompanied each with the matching Draw – you would need to do this if you wanted an outline on your shapes.

```
Protected Overrides Sub OnPaint(ByVal e As System.Windows.Forms.
PaintEventArgs)
   Dim canvas As System.Drawing.Graphics
   canvas = Me.CreateGraphics()
   Dim mypen As New Pen(Color.Black, 4)
   Dim mybrush As New SolidBrush(Color.Blue)
   canvas.FillEllipse(mybrush, 25, 10, 100, 100)
   canvas.DrawEllipse(mypen, 25, 10, 100, 100)
   canvas.FillPie(mybrush, 150, 10, 200, 100, 180, 45)
   canvas.DrawArc(mypen, 150, 10, 200, 100, 180, 45)
   canvas.FillRectangle(mybrush, 50, 150, 200, 75)
   canvas.DrawRectangle(mypen, 50, 150, 200, 75)
End Sub
```

Figure 8.7

Filled shapes with added drawn lines

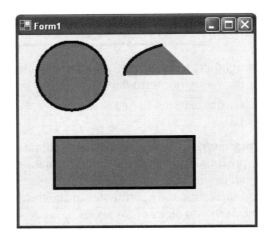

HatchBrush

A hatched fill takes a bit more effort, but can be worth it. The HatchBrush belongs to the `Drawing2D` class, so that must be imported or specified in the line. When creating a new brush, you need to specify the hatch style, and the foreground and background colours – in that order. Hatch styles are easily handled – type 'Drawing2D.HatchStyle.' and the list of possible settings will be presented to you. Colours are defined in the usual way.

```
Dim myBrushH As New
Drawing2D.HatchBrush(Drawing2D.HatchStyle.
DashedHorizontal,Color.Green,Color.Yellow)
```

Type the following lines into your `OnPaint()` method. They will draw a hatch-filled ellipse, with an outline.

```
Dim canvas As System.Drawing.Graphics = Me.CreateGraphics()
Dim myBrush As New Drawing2D.HatchBrush(Drawing2D. HatchStyle.
DashedHorizontal, Color.Green, Color.Yellow)
Dim myPen As New Pen(Color.Black, 4)
canvas.FillEllipse(myBrush, 150, 50, 150, 250)
canvas.DrawEllipse(myPen, 150, 50, 150, 250)
```

Figure 8.8

An ellipse with a hatched fill.

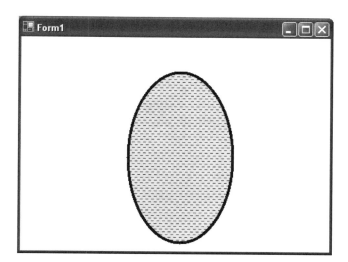

> ### *Task 8.1*
>
> Use the Help system to find out about the other Brush types and draw shapes to demonstrate the range of ways in which they can be filled.

8.4 Worked example: spots before the eyes

This is a trivial program. It scatters circles on the screen at random – at least, the positions and colours are random; the sizes are fixed, but they can also be randomised if you care to add the necessary code. The random colours are produced using the `FromRGB()` function which we will be looking at in section 8.7. Please accept, for the moment, that the expression:

```
...Color.FromArgb(red, green, blue)
```

uses the values in the variables red, green and blue, to define a colour.

One other things to watch out for. The drawing code runs through a loop, and we must have a way out of this. The solution lies in the Boolean variable *active*. This is declared and set to *True* at the very start of the program, and is used as the control variable of the drawing loop. Towards the end of that loop you will see the line:

```
Application.DoEvents()
```

This releases the system to check for any events that may be occurring, and the event we are looking for here is a click – `OnClick()` in the `Overrides` class will pick up any click, not just one on a specific control. When the user clicks, *active* is set to *False*, and the drawing loop comes to a halt.

Notice the *delay* loop. Modern PCs work so rapidly that you normally need to slow visual effects down so that you can see them. The complex calculation that is going on here has no effect on the values in the program, it's just thumb-twiddling to slow down the execution of the program.

```
For delay = 1 To 100000
    x = CInt(Math.Sin(CDbl(y)))
```

This is set for a form of just over 500 pixels square. You can make the form as large as you like, but do adjust the random lines to suit the size.

```
Public Class Form1
   Inherits  System.Windows.Forms.Form
   Dim active As Boolean = True

# Windows Form Designer generated code

   Protected Overrides Sub OnPaint(ByVal e As System.Windows.Forms.
PaintEventArgs)
   Static Dim canvas As System.Drawing.Graphics
   Dim mypen As New Pen(Color.Black, 2)
   Dim mybrush As New SolidBrush(Color.Blue)
   Dim red, green, blue As Integer
   Dim x, y As Integer
   Dim delay As Integer

   canvas = Me.CreateGraphics()
   Do
      red = Int(Rnd() * 256)
      green = Int(Rnd() * 256)
      blue = Int(Rnd() * 256)
```

```
      mybrush.Color = Color.FromArgb(red, green, blue)
      x = Int(Rnd() * 500)
      y = Int(Rnd() * 500)
      canvas.FillEllipse(mybrush, x, y, 50, 50)
      canvas.DrawEllipse(mypen, x, y, 50, 50)
      For delay = 1 To 100000
         x = CInt(Math.Sin(CDbl(y)))
      Next
      Application.DoEvents()
   Loop While active
End Sub

Protected Overrides Sub OnClick(ByVal e As System.EventArgs)
   active = False
End Sub

End Class
```

Figure 8.9

The spots program, with the size set to a 50 pixel circle. What happens if you bring another window to the front while this is running, then bring this one forward again? What activates the OnPaint event?

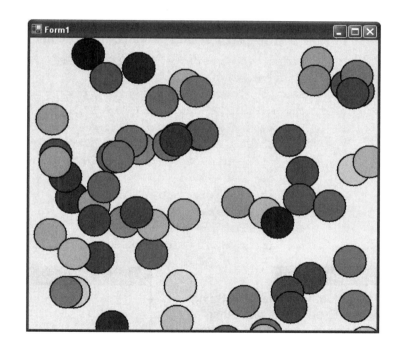

8.5 DrawString()

The DrawString() method writes formatted text on a graphics area. Its syntax is:

> *GraphicsArea*.DrawString(*text, font, brush, x, y*)

where *text* is the text to print, *font* defines the name, size, style, etc. of the font, *brush* sets the colour and *x, y* define the top left corner of the print area on the paper. These can be written directly into the method, or handled through variables.

The font can be specified in great detail – which means it can get quite complicated – but all that is actually essential is the font name and size. The name is a string, and is given as it appears in the Fonts folder or in the Font list of a word processor, e.g. "Arial", "Lucida Bright". Have a look in your folder or Font list to see what is available on your PC (but note that Visual Basic can only handle True Type fonts).

Like pens and brushes, fonts are Graphics objects. They can be constructed in advance, or defined within the drawing method. These two lines:

```
Dim myFont As New Font("Arial", 16)
canvas.DrawString("Test", myFont, myBrush, 100, 100)
```

Have the same effect as this one:

```
canvas.DrawString("Test", New  Font("Arial", 16), myBrush, 100,100)
```

You can see `DrawString()` at work in the next example. It produces the labelled axes for a graph. To write the numbers at the tick marks, you need code like this:

```
canvas.DrawString(tick, myFont, mybrush, tick * 20, 250)
```

In practice, a little adjustment is needed to nudge the text into the right place.

The amount of adjustment depends upon the size (and to a lesser extent the name) of the font and the scale of the ticks – these are drawn 20 pixels apart. Be prepared to alter the values in those lines to suit your display.

```
Protected Overrides Sub OnPaint(ByVal  e  As  System.Windows.Forms.
PaintEventArgs)
   Static Dim canvas As System.Drawing.Graphics
   Dim myFont As New Font("Arial", 10)
   Dim mybrush As New SolidBrush(Color.Black)
   Dim barPen As New Pen(Color.Black, 2)    ' thicker for the axes
   Dim tickPen As New Pen(Color.Black, 1)   ' thin for the tick marks
   Dim tick As Short
   canvas = Me.CreateGraphics()
   ' draw the axes
   canvas.DrawLine(barPen, 50, 250, 250, 250)
   canvas.DrawLine(barPen, 50, 50, 50, 250)
```

Figure 8.10

The output from the DrawString demo. Experiment with other fonts, sizes and ranges of axes.

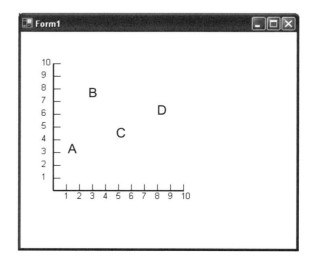

```
For tick = 1 To 10
    ' draw the ticks
    canvas.DrawLine(tickPen, 50 + tick * 20, 250, 50 + tick * 20, 240)
    canvas.DrawLine(tickPen, 50, 250 - tick * 20, 60, 250 - tick * 20)
    ' write the labels
    canvas.DrawString(tick, myFont, mybrush, 45 + tick * 20, 250)
    canvas.DrawString(tick, myFont, mybrush, 30, 240 - tick * 20)
Next
End Sub
```

> ### Task 8.2
>
> Plot these points on your axes, labelling them with their letters: A (10,30),
> B (25,80), C (50,50) and D (85, 70).

8.6 Tidying up drawings

Among the other methods in the Drawing class are two which can be used for
'tidying up' operations – in two senses of the term.

Clear( )

`Clear()` clears the graphics area by filling it with a flat colour – typically the
background colour – erasing any drawing. The syntax is:

`GraphicsArea.Clear(color)`

For example, if the form's BackColor was white, this would clear the area:

`canvas.Clear(Color.White)`

Dispose( )

This does a very different sort of tidying up. When you create a New instance of
any object, it takes up space in memory, and it will continue to occupy that space
after you have finished with it unless you tidy it up. In a busy program, the drain
on memory resources can become a problem. Get into the habit of disposing of
objects when you have finished with them to free up their space.

The syntax is:

`object.Dispose()`

For example, you will find this in the exit routine of the next program:

`myBrush.Dispose()`

8.7 Defining colours

Colours from RGB values

So far we have used the palettes for defining colours at design time and the Color names for defining them during run-time. There are other ways of doing it.

On a computer screen, colours are created by combining red, green and blue light in differing intensities. The value of each light is held in one byte, and so is between 0 and 255, giving you a theoretical range of 256^3 (16+ million) colours. This is 24-bit colour (3 bytes × 8 bits per byte). The `FromArgb()` function allows you to specify a colour from its red, green and blue components. It is used in this form, where *red*, *green* and *blue* are short integer values or variables:

```
...Color.FromArgb(red, green, blue)
```

Here's a short demo program which explores it.

On a form place one PictureBox, called *picCanvas* and three HScrollBars, *hsbRed*, *hsbBlue* and *hsbGreen*, with accompanying Labels.

Figure 8.11

A possible layout for the FromArgb demo program

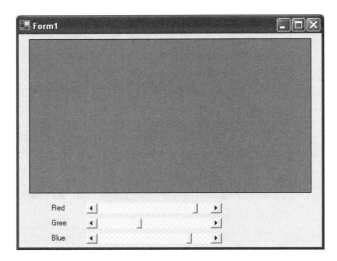

Go to the code window and add this code to the appropriate controls. Note the three general variables that are declared at the top of the program.

```
Public Class Form1
    Inherits System.Windows.Forms.Form
    Dim red, green, blue As Short
    Private Sub Form1_Load(ByVal sender As System.Object, ByVal e As
System.EventArgs) Handles MyBase.Load
      red = 255
      blue = 255
      green = 255
      picCanvas.BackColor = Color.FromArgb(red, green, blue)
End Sub
```

```
    Private Sub hsbRed_Scroll(ByVal sender As System.Object, ByVal e
As System.Windows.Forms.ScrollEventArgs) Handles hsbRed.Scroll
    red = hsbRed.Value
    picCanvas.BackColor = Color.FromArgb(red, green, blue)
End Sub
    Private Sub hsbGreen_Scroll(ByVal sender As System.Object, ByVal e
As System.Windows.Forms.ScrollEventArgs) Handles hsbGreen.Scroll
    green = hsbGreen.Value
    picCanvas.BackColor = Color.FromArgb(red, green, blue)
End Sub
    Private Sub hsbBlue_Scroll(ByVal sender As System.Object, ByVal e As
System.Windows.Forms.ScrollEventArgs) Handles hsbBlue.Scroll
    blue = hsbBlue.Value
    picCanvas.BackColor = Color.FromArgb(red, green, blue)
End Sub
End Class
```

The ColorDialog control

Sliders for each component will give your user good control over colours, but here's another way to give them the same control with far less work on your part!

In the Toolbox you will find controls which produce the standard Windows dialog boxes – including the one for picking a colour. Let's put it to work.

1 Go to the Design window, find the ColorDialog control (it's way down the bottom of the list) and drop it onto the form. It will go into the component tray which will appear at the bottom of the window.

2 Add a Button to the form, and write this code into its Click event.

```
If ColorDialog1.ShowDialog() = DialogResult.OK Then
    picCanvas.BackColor = ColorDialog1.Color
```

3 Build and run the program again. Click the Button and the Color dialog box will open. Pick a colour, click **OK** and your canvas should take that colour.

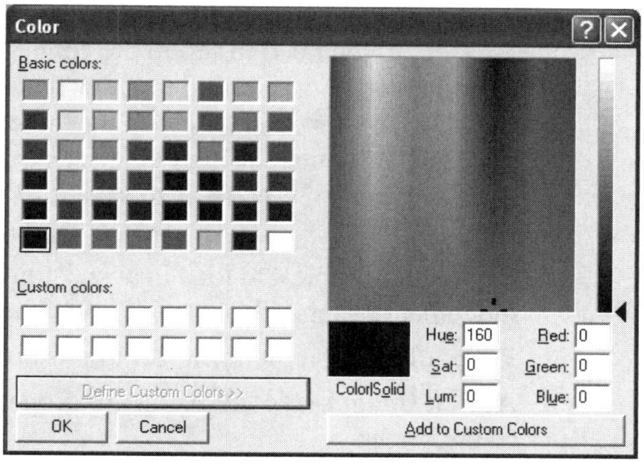

Figure 8.12

The Color dialog box – here shown fully open. It initially appears in its compact form.

Let's look at the code again to see how it worked.

```
If ColorDialog1.ShowDialog() = DialogResult.OK Then
```

The `ShowDialog()` method makes the dialog box appear, but you then need a means of getting the choice from there back to your code. By setting it in an `If` statement and checking for the **OK** result, this picks up the point at which it closes and also ensures that the code only takes the choice if the user has clicked **OK**.

```
    picCanvas.BackColor = ColorDialog1.Color
```

A Color dialog box only has one item of information – its Color property. Some dialog boxes, as you will see in the next chapter, hold several items.

8.8 Working with imported graphics

We first met the idea of assigning graphics to the Image property of controls back in Chapter 2, and have touched on it a few times since. Let's have a closer look at the possibilities of graphics in Visual Basic programs.

Images and ImageLists

Several different types of controls have Image or BackgroundImage properties into which graphics can be imported for display. Some controls, such as Buttons and Labels also have an **ImageList** which can store sets of images. You might, for example, have two alternative images for a Button to represent its normal and 'pushed-in' states. If you are going to do animation, an ImageList offers a convenient place to store the set of images and a convenient way to manage the changes of image when the animation is active – all you need to do is change the index number. For displaying the images, use a Label – not a PictureBox (it won't have an ImageList).

Using an ImageList is basically straightforward – but you have to do things in the right order. The key to handling ImageLists is to realise that all the images in a list will automatically be made the same size, but that you cannot control the size through the ImageList itself – images will either be the size of the control linked to the ImageList or the default 16×16 pixels. Which means that before you start on the ImageList you need to set up the control which will display the images – and when doing that you will need to know the size of the images. Here's the process:

1 Create your first image, cropping the canvas down to the minimum before saving it. (If you are using Paint, select the area which just encloses the image and use **Edit > Copy To...** to save it to file.) Make a note of the size.

2 Create the other images for the set, making sure that they are all the same size – it's often simplest to load in an existing image from the set, edit it to give the movement change, then save it with a new name.

3 Place a **Label** on the form, setting its size to suit the images.

4 Add an **ImageList** control – it will drop into the components tray at the bottom of the screen.

5 Select the **Label**, and set its **ImageList** property to link to the new list.

6 Select the **ImageList** and click the ▣ for the **Image** property to open the Image Collection Editor.

7 Click **Add** to add a new image – you will find it helps if you run the Open dialog box in Thumbnail view so that you can check which image is being added.

Add the images in the same order that they will be used when animated, so that you can cycle through the index to produce smooth animation.

Figure 8.13

Adding images to an ImageList. You should name your images to indicate the type of action and the image's place in the sequence, then store them in the same sequence.

If you add images out of order, or add new ones later, you can rearrange them with the arrow keys – but with only those tiny icons to guide you, it is difficult to see what you are doing.

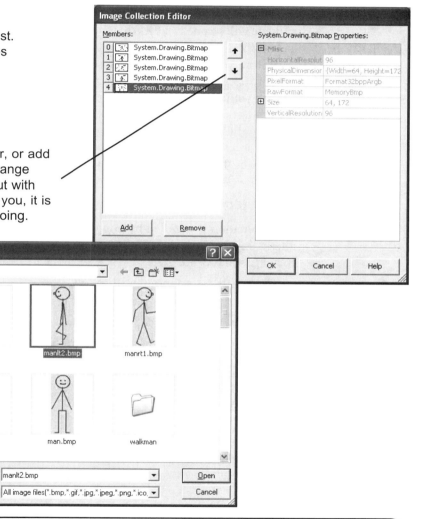

Graphics files

The graphics imported into Pictures can be .bmp (bitmap) or .dib (device independent bitmap), .rle (run length encoded), .wmf (Windows metafile) or .ico (icons). Bitmaps are the simplest to use, as these are the default file types for Paint, which is presumably where you will create your graphics.

8.9 Animation

This next example is ridiculous, trivial and not to be missed. Animation is such a rewarding activity that it drives you to explore deeper into the system in search of better effects. Get this program running, embellish it and extend it, and you will find that you have learnt far more than you would have expected about the interaction between controls and events. As shown here, the program makes a stick man run backwards and forwards across the screen. The animation is crude – but that is merely a reflection of my limitations as an artist. The images that you animate will be ones that you have created, and they can be as colourful and detailed as you like.

Before you can do anything else, you must create a set of graphics to animate. Five are needed for this simple animation – two facing left, two facing right and one standing still. This is an absolute minimum. For smoother movement you need at least three or four images for each step. When the core program is running properly, you might like to extend it to add a third or fourth graphic for each direction. Each picture should be the same size, and no larger than needed – the larger the graphic, the slower the animation. My images are 64×172.

Basic techniques

The animation is handled by copying images from the ImageList into the Label, alternating between two pictures and moving the Image at the same time. The ImageList has 5 images:

Images(0) = first movement to left

Images(1) = second movement to left

Images(2) = first movement to right

Images(3) = second movement to right

Images(4) = standing still

A variable, *manstep*, is flipped between 0 and 1. This is used directly for selecting the image when the man moves to the left, or 2 is added to it for setting the images when moving to the right:

```
If way = "Left" Then
   lblMan.Left = lblMan.Left - 32
   lblMan.Image = ImageList1.Images(manstep)
```

This could easily be extended if there were more than two pictures for each direction. With three alternative images, you would want this:

```
manstep = manStep + 1
If manstep > 2 Then manstep = 0
   ....
   lblMan.Image = ImageList1.Images(manstep)
```

How far to move with each new image depends upon the size and nature of the image. As developed here, where my Man's image is 64 pixels wide, an adjustment of 32 to the Left or Right property produces a reasonable effect. Trial and error is the best way forward.

The whole of the movement routine is run off a Timer. This gives us continuous movement, no matter what else is happening on the form, plus an easy way of adjusting the speed, by linking the Timer Interval to the Scroll Bar.

Form layout

Where you place controls on this form is a matter of choice, and the location of some controls is quite irrelevant.

The ScrollBar should be set up to range from a Min of 10 to a Max of around 200, with an initial Value of 100. (And once again, trial and error will suggest the best limits for your animation.) The value from here will be passed to the Timer's Interval. The Timer is initially turned off. It is enabled by clicking on the *btnLeft* and *btnRight* Buttons.

Figure 8.14

The animation form with the controls in place

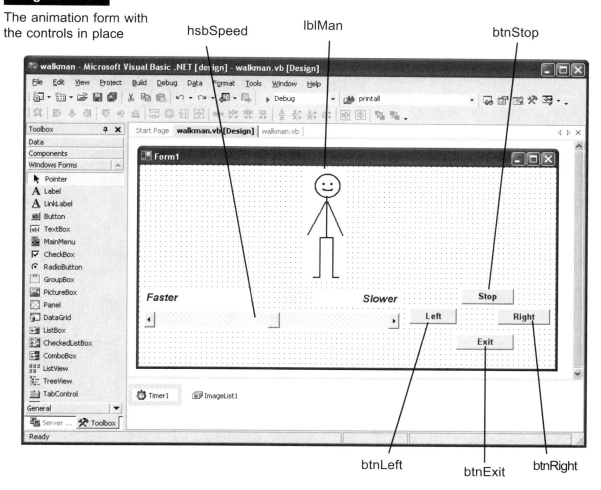

The animation code

It takes remarkably little code to produce simple animation.

- The Left and Right Buttons just set the way and turn the Timer on.
- The Stop Button turns the Timer off and sets the image to the standing man.
- The Slider copies its value, when changed, over to the Timer.
- The Timer moves the Label and changes its image.

```
Public Class Form1
   Inherits  System.Windows.Forms.Form

   Windows Form Designer generated code

   Dim manstep As Short = 0
   Dim way As String = "None"

   Private Sub btnLeft_Click(ByVal eventSender As System.Object,
ByVal eventArgs As System.EventArgs) Handles btnLeft.Click
   way = "Left"
   Timer1.Enabled = True
End Sub
   Private Sub btnRight_Click(ByVal eventSender As System.Object,
ByVal eventArgs As System.EventArgs) Handles btnRight.Click
   way = "Right"
   Timer1.Enabled = True
End Sub
   Private Sub btnStop_Click(ByVal eventSender As System.Object,
ByVal eventArgs As System.EventArgs) Handles btnStop.Click
   Timer1.Enabled = False
   lblMan.Image = ImageList1.Images(4)
End Sub
   Private Sub hsbSpeed_Scroll(ByVal eventSender As System.Object,
ByVal eventArgs As System.Windows.Forms.ScrollEventArgs) Handles
hsbSpeed.Scroll
   Timer1.Interval = hsbSpeed.Value
End Sub
   Private Sub Timer1_Tick(ByVal eventSender As System.Object, ByVal
eventArgs As System.EventArgs) Handles Timer1.Tick
   If manstep = 0 Then
     manstep = 1
   Else
     manstep = 0
   End If
   If way = "Left" Then
```

```
        lblMan.Left = lblMan.Left - 32
        lblMan.Image = ImageList1.Images(manstep)
    Else
        lblMan.Left = lblMan.Left + 32
        lblMan.Image = ImageList1.Images(manstep + 2)
    End If
End Sub
    Private Sub cmdExit_Click(ByVal eventSender As System.Object,
ByVal eventArgs As System.EventArgs) Handles btnExit.Click
    End
End Sub
End Class
```

Figure 8.15

And when you've got it going, do
replace those stick men with some
pictures with a bit more style!

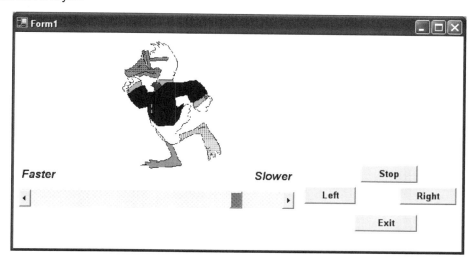

Task 8.3

Create your own set of pictures and animate them as described above. Once
you have the program working at this simple level, either add Up and Down
controls, or adapt it to produce smoother movement. What would you have
to do to give the character a life of its own, so that it could move without being
controlled by Buttons?

8.10 Exercises

8.1 Write a program to draw a simple electrical circuit or other line and block image, labelling the components with `DrawString()`.

8.2 Using the RGB demo as a base, write a program to create a gradient fill, shading from one selected colour across to another by drawing thin lines of steadily changing colours. You will need to record the red, green and blue values of the start and end colours, then calculate the amount of change for each.

8.3 Make a 'flick-book' by creating a set of pictures displaying some kind of activity – a matchstick person doing aerobics, a machine in motion with flashing lights and whirling wheels, the cow jumping over the moon, or whatever. They should all be the same size (the smaller they are, the faster they can be manipulated), and stored in an ImageList. Use a Timer to cycle through them on screen, changing images 10 times a second or faster, looping back to the start after the last has been displayed.

Remember to include some means of stopping the animation, or you could be forced to use **[Ctrl]+[Alt]+[Del]** to reclaim control of your PC!

A possible solution to Exercise 8.2 is given in the Appendix.

9 Arrays and collections

Arrays provide a compact and efficient means of handling blocks of data. Collections of controls can give a similar efficiency to your handling of objects on forms.

9.1 Dimensions, elements and subscripts

Arrays probably add more to the power of programming than any other feature, for they make it possible to process a mass of data through a standard routine. With an array in use, the same procedure will work just as well with 10 or 10,000 items.

An array is a set of variables – of any type – all with the same name, but with different identifying numbers or *subscripts*. A simple one-dimensioned array can be thought of as a numbered list.

Array	Contents
Names(0)	Fred
Names(1)	Jim
Names(2)	Sally
Names(3)	Dick
Names(4)	Karen
Names(5)	Jo

This array would have been set up with the line:

```
Dim Names(6) As String
```

This has 6 *elements*, numbered 0 to 5. Each can be accessed individually, to read or to change its data, by specifying its subscript: e.g.

```
TextBox1.Text = Names(2)      ' displays Sally
Names(4) = Katy               ' replaces Karen with Katy
```

Note that arrays always start at 0, and the highest subscript will be one less than the number in the Dim statement.

A two-dimensional array may be thought of as a table, with numbered rows and columns.

OXO	0	1	2
0	X		
1			
2		O	

This could be the board for Noughts and Crosses. It would be declared with the line:

```
Dim OXO(2,2) As String
```

In the illustration, OXO(0,0) holds "X", and OXO(2,1) holds "O". There is no rule that says you must refer to rows first, then columns. You can think of your array whichever way round you like – as long as you are consistent.

A three-dimensional array gives you a structure like that of a modern spreadsheet, with multiple pages, each containing a grid of cells. And for those arrays with four or more dimensions, you can think up your own analogies. Visual Basic permits you to have up to 60 dimensions, with subscripts ranging from 0 to 2 billion! Memory space is a consideration with large arrays. One with three dimensions, each of 100, has 1,000,000 elements. If it is to hold integers, they will require 2 bytes each; longs and singles take 4 bytes; doubles and currency, 8 bytes; and strings 1 byte per character – plus management overheads.

For example:

```
Dim wages(51,19) As Currency
```

will set up an array to hold the weekly wages of 20 workers, and will require a little over $52 * 20 * 8 = 8320$ bytes, just over 8Kb.

```
Dim marks(10,30,25) As Double
```

This will hold the marks of 10 classes of students, with up to 30 in a class and 25 assignments per student. It will need $10 * 30 * 25 * 8 = 60,000$ bytes of storage.

If the size of the array will not be known at the start of the program – perhaps because it will be up to the users to specify their storage needs – the dimensions can be omitted from the Dim line. They can then be given later, when they are known, with the ReDim statement.

```
Dim yourdata()                      ' in general declarations

ReDim yourdata(rows, cols, pages)   ' in a later procedure
```

Here *rows*, *cols* and *pages* would be variables holding user-defined values.

An array can be ReDimmed any number of times, but note that existing data is lost unless the Preserve option is used, e.g.

```
ReDim Preserve inputdata(rows, cols) ' do not empty array
```

9.2 Arrays and loops

Most data processing in arrays is done through loops, as the routine which works for one element works for all. As the number of elements is known, a For...Next structure usually proves to be the logical choice.

Try this simple demonstration. Attach the *input* and the *results* routines to two Buttons, and set up the array at the top of the code to make it global.

```
Public Class Form1
   Inherits  System.Windows.Forms.Form
   Dim dataset(10) As Single

Windows Form Designer generated code

   Private Sub btnInput_Click(ByVal sender As System.Object, ByVal e
As System.EventArgs) Handles btnInput.Click
   Dim element As Integer
   For element = 0 To 9
     DataSet(element)  = InputBox("Next value?")
   Next element
   End Sub

   Private Sub btnResults_Click(ByVal sender As System.Object, ByVal
e As System.EventArgs) Handles btnResults.Click
   Dim element As Integer
   Dim total, average As Single
   For element = 0 To 9
     total = total + dataset(element)
   Next element
   average = total / 10
   MsgBox("Total values = " & total & " Average = " & average)
End Sub
End Class
```

> **Task 9.1**
>
> Place two more command Buttons on the form and attach to them routines to display the values in the array, and to edit any chosen element.

9.3 Prime numbers

Finding prime numbers has long been a favourite activity of programmers, because finding bigger numbers faster is a demonstration of the power of a computer and of its program. So why don't we join in the fun too. The following program is based on the fact that a prime number cannot be divided evenly by any other. It starts with 2 as the first prime, and works through the number sequence. As it goes, it divides each number by every prime it knows about, discarding any that leave no remainder. The algorithm takes the shape:

```
If num / primes(n)  = Int(num / primes(n)) Then
   primenum = False
```

(The actual program lines are slightly different as the *num* value is held in the Label *lblNum*, so that it can be easily displayed.)

If it reaches the end of the known primes without finding a divisor, then that number is added to the primes set – and the primes are, of course, held in an array.

The program has two limitations, which will prevent you from using it to get into the Guinness Book of Records.

- The first is the size of the array. In the demo program this is set at 1000. You can push this as high as your computer can manage.

- The second limitation is time. The first couple of hundred primes are found in a matter of seconds, but the further you go, the longer it takes to check each number against the ever-growing primes set.

The form layout for this program is shown in Figure 9.1. You will notice that I have included a Stop Button in the design, so that you can halt the search when you grow bored. The Button sets the variable *finished* to True. This causes the search loop to end, and the results to be displayed.

You will also see that there is a Scroll bar on the TextBox used to display the results. To get this, set the TextBox's **ScrollBars** property to *Vertical*. Without the scroll bar, the TextBox could only display the first 300 or so primes.

Figure 9.1

The form layout for the primes program

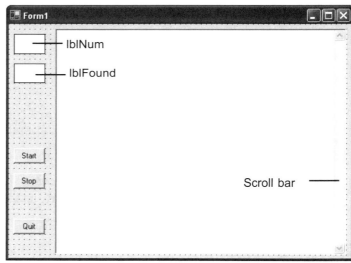

lblNum is used to hold and to display the number currently being checked by the search routine

lblFound is updated as each new prime is identified

```
Public Class Form1
    Inherits System.Windows.Forms.Form
    Dim finished As Boolean

 Windows Form Designer generated code

    Private Sub btnStart_Click(ByVal sender As System.Object, ByVal e As
System.EventArgs) Handles btnStart.Click
    Dim primes(1000) As Integer
    Dim count, num, found As Integer
    Dim primelist As String
    Dim primenum As Boolean
    finished = False
    primelist = "Primes: "          ' header text for display
    num = 2
```

```
lblNum.Text = num                    ' start of number sequence
found = 0
lblFound.Text = found
primes(0) = 2                        ' the first known prime
Do                                   ' search routine loop
   num += 1
   lblNum.Text = num
   primenum = True
   For count = 0 To found            '  divide by known primes
      If num Mod primes(count) = 0 Then
         primenum = False            ' quit when divisor found
         Exit For
      End If
   Next count
   If primenum Then                  ' if no divisor must be prime
      found += 1
      lblFound.Text = found
      primes(found) = num            ' add to primes set
      primelist &= " " & num
   End If
   Application.DoEvents()
   Loop Until finished Or found = 1000
   txtOutput.Text = primelist
End Sub
   Private Sub btnStop_Click(ByVal sender As System.Object, ByVal e
As System.EventArgs) Handles btnStop.Click
   finished = True
End Sub
   Private Sub btnQuit_Click(ByVal sender As System.Object, ByVal e
As System.EventArgs) Handles btnQuit.Click
   End
End Sub
End Class
```

The `Application.DoEvents` statement near the end of the loop returns control, briefly, to the operating system, so that it can check for any Button clicks or other events. Without it, there would be no way of halting the routine, except through **[Ctrl]+[Break]**. Its presence allows the **Stop** procedure to be activated.

Note that the whole purpose of this is to force an exit from the search loop – the flow of execution remains within the `btnStart_Click` procedure, but moves on to display the results.

9.4   Stacks and Reverse Polish arithmetic

A stack is an area of memory accessed on a Last In, First Out basis. In the jargon, data is *pushed* onto a stack and *popped* off it. The operating system and other programs written at machine level use the *Stack* (a predefined part of memory) to track the flow of execution, and for temporary data storage. When the flow goes off from the main code into a sub, the address of the point of leaving is popped onto the stack. If it goes off again from within the sub to another sub or function, the leaving address there is also popped onto the stack – and this can go on for many levels of jumps. When the flow starts to come back out from the subs to the calling code, the address that it needs to go to will be on the top of the stack. This is a very simple but effective means of storing sequences of data.

We will use a simulated stack to hold values in a program that performs calculations using Reverse Polish notation. The first hand-held calculators used this as it is the most efficient way of doing arithmetic – at least, from the program's point of view. In Reverse Polish, operators follow the values on which they are to work, e.g.

```
2   2   +
```

is the same as 2 + 2 in normal notation. With a compound calculation, you start from the leftmost operator, use it on the two previous values, and the result provides one of the values for the next operator. For example, the sum (5 + 4 - 3) * 2 in normal arithmetic becomes this:

```
2   3   4   5   +   -   *       first operation       5   4   +   =   9

2   3   9   -   *               second operation      9   3   -   =   6

2   6   *                       third operation       6   2   *   =   12
```

Implementing it in a program is easy, because there are only two basic rules for the computer to follow as it takes in the string of values and operators:

```
1  If you meet a number, push it on the stack

2  If you meet an operator, pop the last two numbers off the
   stack, use the operator on them and push the result back
   on the stack.
```

If you were writing the program in assembler, you could use the real stack. As we are working in a high-level language, we will need an array to act as a stack. A variable array would do the job, but we would have to find some means of displaying the contents so that we could see what was going on. If we use an array of controls – TextBoxes or Labels – we can store the numbers and display them in one operation.

When we create the array of controls, we will have to specify what they look like and where they will go on the form. We can do this best if the rest of the controls are in place already and we have a clear idea of what sort of controls to use for the array and where they will go.

Start a new project, calling it 'Polish'. Assemble on the form the Labels, TextBoxes and Button as shown in Figure 9.2. *lblNum1*, *lblNum2*, *lblOp* and *lblAnswer* are Labels used to hold and display data during calculations; *txtIn* is a TextBox for collecting the user's inputs; *lblPoint* is a Label that is moved up and down beside the *StackBox* array to indicate the current top of the stack. It is purely decorative and can be omitted.

You cannot put the *StackBox()* controls on the form because they do not exist at design time – these user-defined controls can only be created from within the code. However, they are based on Labels and have all their normal properties, so

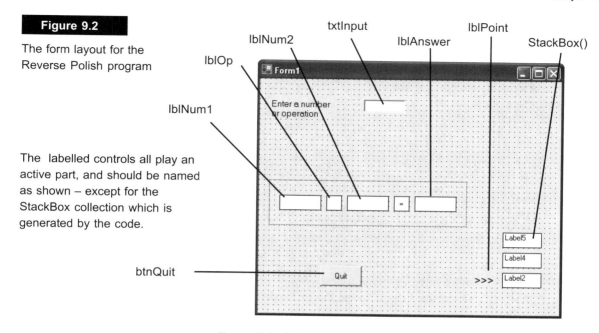

Figure 9.2

The form layout for the
Reverse Polish program

The labelled controls all play an
active part, and should be named
as shown – except for the
StackBox collection which is
generated by the code.

you can use ordinary Labels for planning purposes. Place two or three on the form
at the bottom of the area where the array will go. In my design, the controls are
60×24 pixels and positioned with their Tops 30 pixels apart, and the Left set to
400. Experiment with your Labels, and if you think a different size or layout looks
better, then be prepared to adjust the values later when we write the code for the
control array. When you are happy with the layout, delete the stand-in Labels.

9.5 Collections and control arrays

Up to version 6, Visual Basic offered easy-to-build and easy-to-use control arrays.
These were one of the delights of the language, and not one that existed in the old
programming languages. They allowed you to group and handle controls *en masse*
just as you could handle variables through variable arrays. Unfortunately, in the
move to .Net, this facility has been lost. You can still organise controls into arrays,
but it takes more effect. In the Visual Basic 6 version of the Reverse Polish
program, the array was produced by defining the first Label on the form, then
copying and pasting it a half a dozen times. In the .Net version we have to write a
whole bunch of code to define a new class of objects.

Creating a collection

Visual Basic has a **Collections** class which holds the basic structure and functions
for managing sets of items. To get a control array we have to create a new class of
'collectable' objects, and write code to set their default properties and to provide
a means to add them onto forms and to access them from within the program.

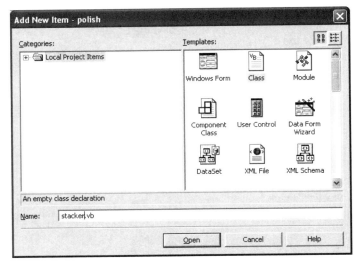

Adding a new class – note
that it has a .vb extension,
the same as a Module.
They are both files of code.

First we have to create a new class.

1 Open the **File** menu and select **Add New Item...**

Or

Open the **Project** menu and select **Add Class ...**

2 At the **Add New Item** dialog box, select **Class** from the **Templates**, give it the
name *Stacker.vb* and click **Open**.

The collection code

An empty class declaration will open in the code window. Type in these lines:

```
Public Class stacker
   Inherits  System.Collections.CollectionBase
   Private ReadOnly HostForm As System.Windows.Forms.Form
```

The first line brings in the core code for collections by linking to the CollectionBase
class. The second creates a Form variable that allows us to link our new control to
the form – I have called it *HostForm*.

We now need to create three procedures. A function to define the new stack/
label object; a New constructor sub to create an instance; and a property to tell us
the index value of the control (i.e. the equivalent of an array subscript).

The AddStack() function

First the function, which I have called `AddStackBox()`. Only these four lines are
absolutely essential:

```
Dim aLabel As New System.Windows.Forms.Label
```

This defines the new control as a Label.

```
Me.List.Add(aLabel)
HostForm.Controls.Add(aLabel)
```

These lines add the object to the internal List of the collection class, and to the set
of controls on the form.

```
      Return aLabel
```

The value returned by this function is an instance of the new aLabel control.

The rest of the code sets the initial properties of the new control, including the **Top** and **Left** to fix its position. You should vary these to suit your layout. Mine all have the Left at 400, and they are space down the screen by this line.

```
      aLabel.Top = 330 - Count * 30
```

Count is the index of the control in the collection's list. This calculation puts aLabel(1) at 300, and aLabel(10) at 30.

Here is the complete code for the function. Set the decorative and size properties however you like.

```
Public Function AddStackBox() As System.Windows.Forms.Label
   ' create a new instance of the Label class
   Dim aLabel As New System.Windows.Forms.Label
   ' add the label to the collection's internal list
   Me.List.Add(aLabel)
   ' add the label to the controls collection of the form
   HostForm.Controls.Add(aLabel)
   ' set initial properties for the label object
   aLabel.Top = 330 - Count * 30      ' stack from the bottom (max 10)
   aLabel.Left = 400
   aLabel.BackColor = Color.White
   aLabel.BorderStyle = BorderStyle.FixedSingle
   aLabel.Width = 60
   aLabel.Height = 24
   Return aLabel
End Function
```

You do not have to set the new control's properties at this point. It works here because we know how and where we want the controls to appear. A more flexible approach would be to leave all the properties at their standard defaults, then define them within the calling control. Alternatively, properties could be passed in through parameters, like this:

```
Public Function AddStackBox(ByVal y As Single, ByVal x As Single)
As System.Windows.Forms.Label
   ...
   aLabel.Top = y
   aLabel.Left = x
   ...
```

The call to AddStackBox(x, y) would take in the positional values from the code.

The **New()** constructor

This takes the shape:

```
Public Sub New(ByVal host As System.Windows.Forms.Form)
   HostForm = host
   Me.AddStackBox()
End Sub
```

This links the form in the calling code (*host*) to the form variable (*HostForm*), then uses the AddStackBox() function to add a new aLabel control to it.

The **Item Index** property

The last thing we need to do is ensure that the index value of the control is accessible from the main code. This does the trick.

```
Default Public ReadOnly Property Item(ByVal Index As Integer) As
System.Windows.Forms.Label
    Get
    Return CType(Me.List.Item(Index), System.Windows.Forms.Label)
    End Get
    End Property
End Class
```

Adding controls to the form

There are two steps to this: the first is to the stack array as a variable at the top of the form, using the New constuctor to create an instance of the object.

```
Dim Stack As stacker = New stacker(Me)
```

This also places the first of the boxes on the form. The rest of the stack are added when the form loads, using the `AddStackBox()` function.

```
Private Sub Form1_Load(ByVal sender As System.Object, ByVal e As
System.EventArgs) Handles MyBase.Load
    Dim n As Short
    For n = 1 To 9
        Stack.AddStackBox()
    Next
End Sub
```

That's it. Now let's have a look at the rest of the code.

Code design

The code breaks conveniently into two blocks – one attached to *txtInput* to collect the inputs, and a free-standing procedure to handle the calculations. The *txtInput* code will run off the `KeyPress` event, when [Enter] is pressed. Its design follows the rules set out earlier, with a little extra to prevent stack overflow and to move the pointer.

The structure diagram
for handling inputs

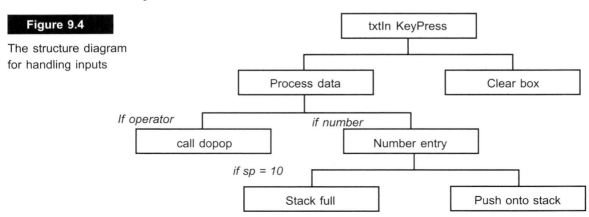

The stack pointer, that tracks the progress through the *Stack* array, has to be accessed by this and the calculating procedure. It is held in the global variable *sp* declared at the top of the program.

The code is a simple translation of the design. You will almost certainly have to adjust the value in the line that moves *lblPoint*, as this depends entirely on the size of the *lblStack* controls. Mine were 30 pixels apart.

```
Private Sub txtInput_KeyPress(ByVal sender As Object, ByVal e As
System.Windows.Forms.KeyPressEventArgs) Handles txtInput.KeyPress
   Dim input As String
   If e.KeyChar <> Chr(13) Then Exit Sub
   ' only process after Enter pressed
   input = txtInput.Text        ' copy to a variable for easier handling
   txtInput.Text = ""           ' clear the input
   If input = "+" Or input = "-"Or input = "*" Or input = "/" Then
      dopop(input)
   ElseIf IsNumeric(input) Then
      If sp = 10 Then                       ' if there are 10 in the array
         MsgBox("Stack overflow", 48)
      Else
         Stack.Item(sp).Text = input        ' push number onto stack
         sp += 1                            ' move the stack pointer
         lblPoint.Top -= 30                 ' and the arrow display
      End If
   End If
End Sub
```

The pop-and-calculate design can be simplified to this:

Figure 9.5

The structure diagram for the calculation code

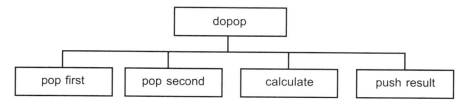

The implementation is a little more complex. We should check that we haven't reached the bottom of the stack before attempting to pop; and the different 'calculate' operations must be handled by a set of Ifs or a Case structure. The whole routine could have been included in the KeyPress code, but splitting it off into a separate procedure makes the program more readable.

```
Private Sub dopop(ByVal op As String)
   Dim num1, num2, answer As Single
   ' pop the first number
   If sp = 0 Then                           ' check for overruntrap
      MsgBox("Bottom of stack ", 48)
      Exit Sub
   End If
   sp -= 1                                  ' move the stack pointer
   lblPoint.Top += 30                       ' and the arrow display
```

```
lblNum1.Text = Stack.Item(sp).Text      ' pop the first number
num1 = Val(lblNum1.Text)                 ' copy into variable
Stack.Item(sp).Text = ""                 ' clear the stack box

' pop the second number - identical routine
If sp = 0 Then
   MsgBox("Bottom of stack ", 48)
   Exit Sub
End If
sp -= 1                                  ' move the stack pointer
lblNum2.Text = Stack.Item(sp).Text       ' pop the second number
num2 = Val(lblNum2.Text)                 ' copy into variable
Stack.Item(sp).Text = ""                 ' clear the stack box
lblOp.Text = op
Select Case op
   Case "+" : answer = num1 + num2
   Case "-" : answer = num1 - num2
   Case "*" : answer = num1 * num2
   Case "/" : answer = num1 / num2
End Select
LblAnswer.Text = answer
Stack.Item(sp).Text = answer             ' push the answer onto the stack
sp += 1                                  ' move the display pointer
End Sub
```

If you have placed a 'Quit' Button on the form, it will need an 'End' written into its Click event handler.

Build and run the program. Test it with the sequence we looked at earlier:

```
2  3  4  5  +  -  *
```

This should display 12 after the '*' has been processed. If that test works, try some more – but keep them simple as you should be checking them by hand or with a calculator as part of the testing.

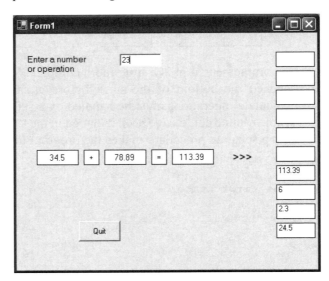

Figure 9.6

The Reverse Polish form in use

9.6 The tabindex and event handling

Here's another way to handle multiple objects with one block of code. There are two aspects to this and both start in the same place. Go into the code window and look at the header line for any Click event handler. First look inside the brackets where you will see this argument:

```
...(ByVal sender As System.Object..)
```

The `sender` identifies the object that was clicked, and part of this identification is its `tabindex` property (normally used to set the order in which objects take the focus when the user presses [Tab]). If you had a set of controls – ordinary ones, not in an array, but with the tabindex values arranged in order – the expression `sender.tabindex` would identify which had been clicked.

This leads us to the second point. Look at the end of the header line of an event handler and you will see something to this effect:

```
... Handles Button1.Click
```

An event handler can be made to handle any number of events by adding their names at the end of the line.

```
... Handles Button1.Click, Button2.Click, Button3.Click...
```

Put those two together and you have the equivalent of a control array, but using standard controls from the Toolbox. The main extra work is in setting the tabindex property of the controls to get them into order, and writing their events into your handler's header line. Where there are relatively few controls, this approach can be more efficient as you can set up the form on screen, and there is less code to write. Once you get over a dozen, the balance tends to shift in favour of the control array.

As a demonstration of using the tabindex and of multiple event handling, here is a simple on-screen calculator. The number Buttons have their **tabindex** property set to match their displayed value (and their names).

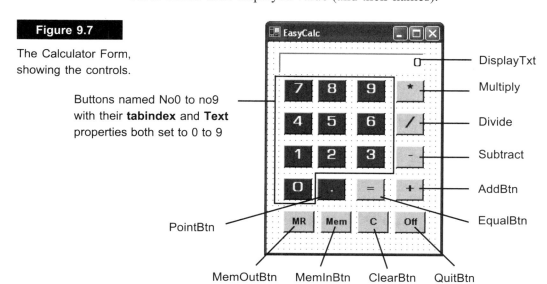

Figure 9.7

The Calculator Form, showing the controls.

Buttons named No0 to no9 with their **tabindex** and **Text** properties both set to 0 to 9

PointBtn

DisplayTxt
Multiply
Divide
Subtract
AddBtn
EqualBtn

MemOutBtn   MemInBtn   ClearBtn   QuitBtn

Here is the most efficient way to set up this form:

1 Open a new project.

2 Place a Button to make the '0' key – as the first control on the form it will have a **tabindex** of 0.

3 Adjust its size, font and colours to suit yourself, then copy it and paste it repeatedly to create the other number 'keys'.

4 Work through the key Buttons in their tabindex order, setting their **Text** to display the appropriate number. The rest of their properties will already have ben set.

5 Add the rest of the Buttons and other controls in any order – their tabindex values are not relevant.

Setting the tabindex

If you do not create your controls in the required order, you can change the tabindex property – it is just a matter of typing in a new value. If this means that a key Button and another control will have the same tabindex, that will not affect the program – the code only use the tabindexes of the keys.

Handling the number keys

A Click on a *digit* can mean either start a new number, or add another figure to the number that is building in the display. We can handle this by having a variable, *newnum*, which is set to *True* when an operator is clicked, after which the user will be starting a new number. *newnum* must be declared as a global variable.

The pseudocode – the structured program outline – is:

```
If it's a new number
   make that the first digit of the number
   turn off the newnum variable
else
   add the digit to the end of the existing number
```

Let's convert this to code. The first job is to set up a sub that can handle the Click events for all the number key Buttons. Try this:

1 Double-click on the '0' key to get into its `Click` event handler. It should read:

```
Private Sub No0_Click(ByVal sender As System.Object, ByVal e As
System.EventArgs) Handles No0.Click
```

2 Add 'No1.Click, No2.Click…No9.Click' to the end of the line. If you want to change its name, do so – it won't make any difference, but it is useful to remind yourself that this doesn't just handle `No0.Click`. Mine looks like this:

```
Private Sub NoButs(ByVal sender As System.Object, ByVal e As
System.EventArgs) Handles No0.Click, No1.Click, No2.Click, No3.Click,
No4.Click, No5.Click, No6.Click, No7.Click, No8.Click, No9.Click
```

We can pick up the digit that the key represents from the `sender.tabindex`. Our pseudocode can then be translated to this:

```
If newnum Then
   DisplayTxt.Text = sender.tabindex     ' start a new number
   newnum = False
Else
   DisplayTxt.Text &= sender.tabindex    ' add a digit to the number
End If
```

The Point Button has to be dealt with separately, but follows the same pattern.

```
Private Sub PointBtn_Click(ByVal sender As System.Object, ByVal e
As System.EventArgs) Handles PointBtn.Click
   If newnum Then
      DisplayTxt.Text = "."
      newnum = False
   Else
      DisplayTxt.Text &= "."
   End If
End Sub
```

Handling the operators

This is a little more complex, and we must stop for a moment and think about how a real pocket calculator is used. When an operator is selected, it is not acted upon immediately, but is put on hold until after the next number has been entered and the next operator selected. Take the sequence: 12 + 34 = When the calculator meets '+' it will store the 12 and make a note that there is an add to do. Only when it reaches '=' will it do the sum.

To do the job properly, we should take *priority* into account. Where there is a sequence of operations, each should only be performed when the next is entered – or possibly not even then, if the current operation has higher priority than the previous one. Multiplication and division should be performed before addition and subtraction; powers, roots and other functions have higher priority than arithmetic operators. (Contrast this with the simplicity of Reverse Polish calculation.) That's if we were doing the job properly – we are not, as this is only intended as a demonstration of handling multiple events.

The pseudocode for the operators takes the form:

```
1 If there is no number available (i.e. the last operator was =
     or we have just started)
   store the operator
2 If there is no operator in store
     store the number in the display
   Else
      get the second number from the display
      do the appropriate calculation
      store operator for next time
3 set the newnum variable to True
```

The code is, of course, virtually the same for all the operators – the only difference is in the calculation. It makes sense to handle it all in one procedure with a Case or If structure to perform the different calculations. Which begs the question, how will the code know which operator was clicked?

We could set up a multiple event handler, with a header line something like this:

```
Private Sub Opertors(ByVal sender As System.Object, ByVal e As
System.EventArgs) Handles AddBtn.Click, Subtract.Click, Multiply.Click,
Divide.Click, EqualBtn.Click
```

And in the code we could use the Text on the Buttons to select the Case action:

```
Select Case sender.Text
   Case "+" : n1 += n2
```

That would work. However, I've taken a different approach – just to show that there's often another way! In this program, all operators are processed by one sub, called *processOp()*. This takes as a parameter a number which identifies the operation – Add is 1, Subtract is 2, etc.

```
Private Sub processOp(ByVal operator As Short)
. . .
   Select Case op
      Case 1 : n1 += n2
```

The operator Buttons simply pass the appropriate number to it. Here, for example, is the AddBtn code.

```
Private Sub AddBtn_Click(ByVal sender As System.Object, ByVal e As
System.EventArgs) Handles AddBtn.Click
   processOp(1)
End Sub
```

Here is the complete code for the operators:

```
Private Sub processOp(ByVal operator As Short)
   If newnum Then        ' if last operator was = and no number yet
      op = operator       ' entered then simply store next operator
      Exit Sub
   End If
   If (op = 0) Or (op = 5) Then
      ' no operation yet recorded - first number in display
      n1 = Val(DisplayTxt.Text)
      op = operator
   Else
      n2 = Val(DisplayTxt.Text)
      ' process the operator entered between the numbers
      Select Case op
         Case 1 : n1 += n2
         Case 2 : n1 -= n2
         Case 3 : n1 *= n2
         Case 4 : n1 /= n2
      End Select
      DisplayTxt.Text = n1
      op = operator                  ' store operator
   End If
   newnum = True
End Sub
```

```
   Private Sub AddBtn_Click(ByVal sender As System.Object, ByVal e As
System.EventArgs) Handles AddBtn.Click
      processOp(1)
End Sub
   Private Sub Subtract_Click(ByVal sender As Object, ByVal e As
System.EventArgs) Handles Subtract.Click
     processOp(2)
End Sub
   Private Sub Multiply_Click(ByVal sender As Object, ByVal e As
System.EventArgs) Handles Multiply.Click
     processOp(3)
End Sub
   Private Sub Divide_Click(ByVal sender As Object, ByVal e As
System.EventArgs) Handles Divide.Click
     processOp(4)
End Sub
   Private Sub EqualBtn_Click(ByVal sender As System.Object, ByVal e
As System.EventArgs) Handles EqualBtn.Click
     processOp(5)
End Sub
```

The number values and the operator are only actively used inside this procedure, but must be accessible to *ClearBtn*, so that they can be reset. Their variables must be declared at the global level. Others needed here are *newnum*, which we met earlier, and *memory*, which we will get to shortly.

```
Dim n1, n2 As Double
Dim op As Short
Dim newnum As Boolean = True
Dim memory As Double
```

The code for the four Buttons across the bottom of the calculator is all quite straightforward.

ClearBtn wipes the display and the stored numbers and sets *newnum* to *True*, ready for the first new number.

```
   Private Sub ClearBtn_Click(ByVal sender As System.Object, ByVal e
As System.EventArgs) Handles ClearBtn.Click
   DisplayTxt.Text = ""
   n1 = 0
   n2 = 0
   newnum = True
End Sub
```

MemInBtn copies the displayed value into the memory variable, and again sets *newnum* to *True* – we expect to start a new number after storing one in memory.

```
   Private Sub MemInBtn_Click(ByVal sender As System.Object, ByVal
e As System.EventArgs) Handles MemInBtn.Click
      memory = Val(DisplayTxt.Text)
      newnum = True
End Sub
```

MemOutBtn is almost the exact reverse. It copies the value from the memory into the display, and sets *newnum* to *False*.

```
      Private Sub MemOutBtn_Click(ByVal sender As System.Object, ByVal
e As System.EventArgs) Handles MemOutBtn.Click
          DisplayTxt.Text = memory
          newnum = False
End Sub
```

And finally, there is our normal Exit routine.

```
      Private Sub ExitBtn_Click(ByVal sender As System.Object, ByVal e
As System.EventArgs) Handles ExitBtn.Click
          End
      End Sub
```

9.7 Exercises

9.1 Add code to the total and average program example given in Section 9.2, so that it will:
(1) display the contents of the array;
(2) allow the user to change the value held in any element;
(3) work out the maximum and minimum values in the set;
(4) sort the set into order.

9.2 Design and write a program that will take a set of 10 numbers and convert them into a bar chart and/or pie chart display. For a decent bar chart, you must scale your values to make best use of the available space. Before drawing the bars, find the largest number in the set and use this and the height of the display area to work out a suitable scale factor.

9.3 Design and write a program to create a Noughts and Crosses board. The board should be made from an array of 9 TextBoxes. Players will enter their move by clicking on a square and typing X or O. The program should check for completed lines and for a full board and announce the winner or a draw.

Add a procedure to the Noughts and Crosses game so that the computer can play a sensible game.

Possible solutions to Exercise 9.1, 9.2 and 9.3 are given in the Appendix.

10 Multiple forms and windows

So far our projects have been built in one form and run in a single window, but one of the features of Windows programs is that they can run any number of separate windows outside or within the main application window.

10.1 A second form

Additional windows are produced by adding forms, and it can be done in two ways:

- With the second and subsequent forms opening outside the main form. These are dependent on the main form – you can open and close secondary forms without affecting anything else, but if the main form is closed, the application ends. The Save, Open and other dialog boxes are actually forms of this type.

- With additional forms opening inside the main form, as document windows. These are MDI (Multiple Document Interface) forms, and they have a distinct *parent–child* relationship.

In either case, similar techniques are used for setting up and handling multiple forms, but MDI forms are slightly more work to set up, while free-standing forms are a bit trickier to manage.

Figure 10.1

Starting to add a form

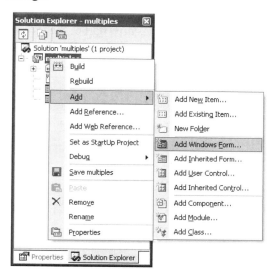

To add a form:

1 Open the **File** menu and select **Add New Item...**

Or

Open the **Project** menu and select **Add Windows Form...**

Or

In the Solution Explorer, right-click on the project name. In the context menu, point to **Add** and select **Add Windows Form...**

2 All routes lead to the **Add New Item** dialog box. Make sure that **Windows Form** is selected.

3 If you wish to give the form a more meaningful name, do so – if you have several forms, renaming them is a good idea.

4 Click **Open**.

The form can then have controls added as needed, just as with a normal form.

Figure 10.2

If you start from the Project menu or the context menu, Windows Form will be selected

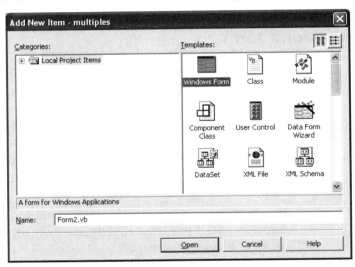

Though the form is now part of the project, it is not yet linked to the main form. This is done through the code. Let's try it.

1 If you have not already done so, start a new project and add a form to it – you can leave the name as *Form2*.

2 On the main form add a Button, with the text 'Go to Form2'.

3 On Form2 add a Button with the text, 'Back to Form1'.

10.2 Code for multiple forms

Secondary forms are brought into the main one by declaring them as variables. In fact, you do not link to the form itself, but instead create a new instance of it. The code has this shape:

```
Dim variable As New Formname
```

If the secondary form is only accessed from one subroutine, then the `Dim` line can be written in there, otherwise it should be declared globally at the top of the code or in a module. In this example, we can write it into the Button's Click sub.

Double-click on the Button to open the Code window and type:

```
Dim F2 As New Form2        ' or whatever you called your form
```

The form can now be referenced through the variable, *F2*. If required, you can read or set the properties of elements on that form from within the main form. For example, you could change the text on the title bar with the line:

```
F2.Text = "The new form"
```

When the program starts, the form will not be visible – it does not in fact exist until created with `Dim`. To make it visible, use the `Show()` or `ShowDialog()` method. Add this to the Button code:

```
F2.Show()
```

While the window is active, the user can switch between the two by clicking on them.

When you have finished with a secondary form you can `Hide()` it or `Close()` it to return to the main form.

Double-click on *Form2*'s Button and type this into its Click sub:

```
Me.Hide()
```

How many forms?

With a straightforward `Dim` declaration, a new instance of the form will be produced if the routine is activated again. This will not be obvious on screen, as the windows will open in exactly the same place every time, directly on top of the existing ones.

If you want to have only one instance of the secondary window, use `Static` in your declaration.

```
Static Dim F2 As New Form2
```

10.3 Modules and global variables

If there are several secondary forms and you want to be able to pass data between them, or if you want to be able to use the same subroutines or functions from different forms, you need a *module*. This is a separate file, and code stored in here can be accessed from any other part of the project.

To create a module:

1 Open the **Project** menu and select **Add Module...** or start from **File** menu or the context menu in Solution Explorer.

2 In the **Add New Item** dialog box, select **Module** (if neccessary), change the name if required and click **Open**.

If you want to set up a form so that it can be accessed from anywhere in the project, declare it at the top of the code, using the `Public` keyword instead of `Dim`, e.g.

```
Public F2 as Form2
```

To make a subroutine or function globally-accessible, write it here. Try it. Type in the `proper()` function that we developed in Chapter 7:

```
Private Function proper(ByVal incoming As String) As String
    proper = UCase(Mid(incoming, 1, 1)) & LCase(Mid(incoming, 2))
End Function
```

Now add a TextBox and a Button to each of the forms, adding this code to the Button (changing the TextBox name if need be):

```
TextBox1.Text = proper(TextBox1.Text)
```

10.4 A two-form project

This next project is a simple example of a multi-window application. It also shows how you can set up one subroutine so that it handles events generated by several controls. The main form has six PictureBoxes into which images can be loaded from file, and where they are displayed as thumbnails. A click on any PictureBox will open the second form where its image will be displayed full size.

1 Start a new project.

2 Place a PictureBox at Location (0, 0) of Size 160, 120. (If you use a different size, adjust the other locations to suit.)

Figure 10.3

The main form with its controls

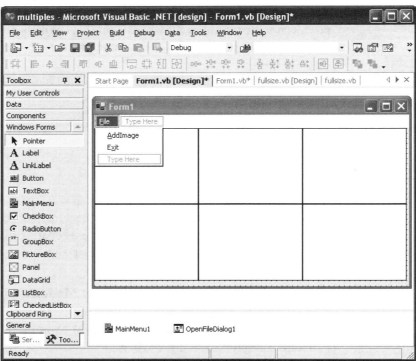

3 Set these properties:

```
Border = FixedSingle
SizeMode = StretchImage
Visible = False
```

4 Copy the PictureBox. Paste it five times, locating the new boxes at (160, 0), (320, 0), (0, 120), (160, 120) and (320, 120).

5 Set up a menu with two items: Add Image and Exit.

6 Add an OpenFileDialog – you'll need it for loading images.

To set up the second form:

1 From the Project menu select Add Windows Form… and complete the dialog box to add the form.

2 Place a PictureBox, setting these properties:

```
SizeMode = CenterImage
Dock = Fill
```

3 Add a Button, with the Text 'Close Window'.

Figure 10.4

The second form

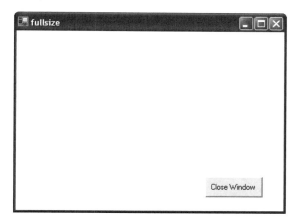

Let's turn to the code to set this all going. Note that I have named the PictureBoxes as PicBox1 to PicBox6, and the two menu items have been named to match their text, but that otherwise the controls are all at their default names.

Two of the routines need a little explanation.

Adding images

To load an image from file into a PictureBox, you need to use the method Image.FromFile() in code like this:

```
PictureBox1.Image = Image.FromFile(filename)
```

To get the filename, we use the OpenFileDialog, as we did for text in section 6.4, but setting its Filter to 'Image files | *.bmp'.

The tricky bit is knowing which PictureBox to load it into. I have set up a *count* variable, which is in a `Select Case` structure to direct the file into the next available PictureBox.

```
Select Case count
   Case 0
      PicBox1.Image = Image.FromFile(filename)
      PicBox1.Visible = True
```

After each addition, the count is incremented, but kept within the range 0 to 5.
Here's the code for the Form_Load and for each of the menu commands for Form1.

```
Public Class Form1
   Inherits  System.Windows.Forms.Form
   Dim filename As String
   Dim count As Short
# Windows Form Designer generated code
   Private  Sub  Form1_Load(ByVal  sender  As  System.Object,  ByVal  e  As
System.EventArgs)  Handles  MyBase.Load
   count = 0
End Sub
   Private Sub FileAddImage_Click(ByVal sender As System.Object, ByVal e As
System.EventArgs)  Handles  FileAddImage.Click
   OpenFileDialog1.Filter = "Image files |*.bmp"
   If OpenFileDialog1.ShowDialog = DialogResult.OK Then
      filename = OpenFileDialog1.FileName
   Else
      Exit Sub                    ' no image file to add
   End If
   Select Case count
      Case 0
         PicBox1.Image = Image.FromFile(filename)
         PicBox1.Visible = True
      Case 1
         PicBox2.Image = Image.FromFile(filename)
         PicBox2.Visible = True
      Case 2
         PicBox3.Image = Image.FromFile(filename)
         PicBox3.Visible = True
      Case 3
         PicBox4.Image = Image.FromFile(filename)
         PicBox4.Visible = True
      Case 4
         PicBox5.Image = Image.FromFile(filename)
         PicBox5.Visible = True
      Case 5
         PicBox6.Image = Image.FromFile(filename)
         PicBox6.Visible = True
   End Select
   count += 1                              ' increment the count
   If count > 5 Then count = 0
End Sub
   Private Sub FileExit_Click(ByVal sender As System.Object, ByVal e As
System.EventArgs)  Handles  FileExit.Click
  End
End Sub
```

Displaying images on Form2

Once a form has been declared as a variable, its components can be accessed, so the image in *PicBox1* could be copied into the PictureBox on the second form and displayed with the lines:

```
f2.PictureBox1.Image = PicBox1.Image
f2.Show()
```

Similar code would then be needed on the other five PictureBoxes. You would also have to think about where to declare the form variable. You could declare *f2* in each of the subroutines, which would give you a new window for every image. If you only wanted the one secondary window, then you would declare it at the top of the code.

There is, however, an alternative approach. We can set up a sub to act as event handler for several controls. Here's how.

1   Go to the Design window for the main form.

2   Double-click on PicBox1 to get into its Click subroutine.

3   At the end of the Sub declaration line, after 'Handles PicBox1.Click' add ', PicBox2.Click, PicBox3.Click...' and so on. Notice those commas between the event names.

4   Edit the Sub's name to remind you that it doesn't just handle PicBox1.Click. You should have something like this:

```
Private Sub PicBoxes_Click(ByVal sender As System.Object, ByVal e
As System.EventArgs) Handles PicBox1.Click, PicBox2.Click, PicBox3.
Click, PicBox4.Click, PicBox5.Click, PicBox6.Click
```

How do we know which Picbox has been clicked? The answer is in the parameter *sender*, which identifies the object that generated the Click event. The expression *sender.Image* will pick the Image property out of the clicked PicBox.

Here's the rest of the code for this subroutine.

```
Dim f2 As New Form2
f2.PictureBox1.Image = sender.Image
f2.Show()
End Sub
```

The code on Form2

There is not a lot of this. All we need is a **Close**() method on the 'Close Window' Button. Here is the entire code for the second form.

```
Public Class Form2
   Inherits System.Windows.Forms.Form
# Windows Form Designer generated code
   Private Sub Button1_Click(ByVal sender As System.Object, ByVal e As
System.EventArgs) Handles Button1.Click
   Me.Close()
End Sub
End Class
```

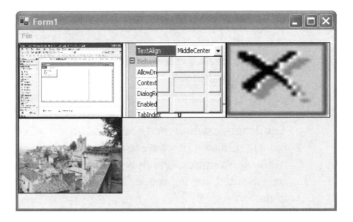

Figure 10.5

The form in action. Only six images can be displayed at any one time, but you can use a larger form, or smaller PictureBoxes and set it up to handle more.

10.5 MDI forms

With MDI (Multiple Document Interface) forms, the main form is known as the *parent*, and a secondary form is referred to as a *child* – and there are properties that control and describe the relationships. When declaring a new child form, for example, it is linked to the parent by a line like this:

```
NewChild.MDIParent = Me      'Me is the parent form
```

The child windows open inside the main window, and this has a number of implications:

- The parent window can have no content, apart from a menu and a toolbar – you must have one or the other to allow you to do anything.
- If there may be more than one child window, you will need routines to manage their layout – but happily there are ready-made commands for the standard Cascade and Tile layouts.
- If you have menus in both the parent and child windows, you will need to ensure that they fit together in some way.

Parent and child forms

To turn a form into a parent form, you simply set its **IsMdiContainer** property to true – you will find it in the Window Style set, towards the bottom of the list.

Do this before you do anything else at all with the form! The central area, where controls are placed, will be emptied to create the space where the child windows will open.

IsMdiContainer is towards the bottom of the Form's properties list

A child form is created in exactly the same way as an ordinary secondary form. It will become a child only when the form is defined in the code, by setting its **MdiParent** property to *Me* – the defining form. The crucial lines look like this:

```
Dim NewChild As New ChildForm
' set the parent form
NewChild.MdiParent = Me
' display the new form
NewChild.Show()
```

A child window can be easily accessed from the parent. For example, in the Open routine, you will see this line:

```
NewChild.Workspace.LoadFile(OpenFileDialog1.FileName)
```

This is virtually the same command that we used to load a file into our text editor. The only difference is that the *Workspace* object is prefixed by *NewChild*, the name of the window.

As there can be any number of child windows, you may need to identify which one you are working with. The parent form has an **ActiveMdiChild** property that knows which child is on top. You can see this at work in the Close routine.

```
Private Sub CloseChild()
   Dim activeChild As Form = Me.ActiveMdiChild
   If activeChild Is Nothing Then Exit Sub
   activeChild.Close()             ' close the window
   activeChild.Dispose()           ' reclaim the memory
End Sub
```

10.6 Menus in MDI forms

In a typical parent–child application you will have two distinct sets of commands. When no child window is open, you only need to be able to open a file, start a new one or exit from the program. Once you have one or more child windows open, you also need to be able to create and edit the document, save the file and manage the window layout.

You can put all your commands in the parent window, and leave the child set disabled until a child window is opened. This works, but there is a neater solution. We can write the commands into a menu on the child form, but merge this with the main form's menu at run-time. It cuts out the need to enable and disable the commands as child windows open and close, but also it lets us place the code *for* the child form *on* the child form. (If your code is trying to access a child form from the main form, it must first work out which child is active, and then include its name when identifying any controls or variables on the form.) There are two aspects to merging menus:

- the menu items which are present in both menus – i.e. the headings – must be put into merge mode;
- the items in the merged menus must be given numbers to indicate their order.

An example will show how this works.

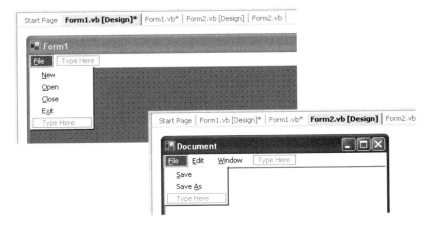

Figure 10.6

Starting to build a merged menu. The menus are created as normal, but with the addition of MergeOrder numbers and with MergeType set to MergeItems

1 Set up **File** menus on both forms. On the parent form place the items **New**, **Open**, **Close** and **Exit**; on the child form, place **Save** and **Save As**.

2 On the parent form, select the **File** item. In the Properties list, set its **MergeType** to *MergeItems* and the **MergeOrder** to *1* – this is the first heading across the menu bar.

3 Work down the **File** menu, setting the **MergeOrder** values to **New** = *1*, **Open** = *2*; **Close** = *3*; **Exit** = *6*. These will be their places in the merged File menu.

4 On the child form, set the **File** item's **MergeType** to *MergeItems* and the **MergeOrder** to *1* – the same as in the other menu.

5 On the child **File** menu, set the **MergeOrder** values **Save** = *4* and **Save As** = *5* so that they slot between **Close** and **Exit**.

Figure 10.7

When a child window is opened, its menu items are merged into the parent's menu according to the MergeOrder

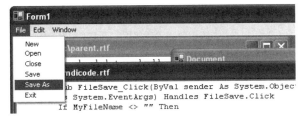

10.7 Window management

Visual Basic makes this very simple. For a start, if you have a **Window** menu item in a parent/child program, it will automatically add to it the names of windows as they are opened. Clicking on them will switch control between the windows, as normal. And you do not have to write a single word of code to make this happen!

Controlling the layout is not much work either. There are three commands, in the **MdiLayout** set which will arrange the child windows in the **Cascade**, **TileHorizontal** and **TileVertical** layouts. These work on the LayoutMdi property of the parent form, but the code is best written on the child form – as they are to be called up by items on the child's Window menu.

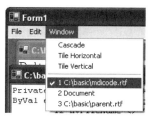

The lines should take this shape:

```
Me.ParentForm.LayoutMdi(MdiLayout.Cascade)
```

or

```
Me.ParentForm.LayoutMdi(MdiLayout.TileHorizontal)
```

or

```
Me.ParentForm.LayoutMdi(MdiLayout.TileVertical)
```

10.8 An MDI text editor

The Parent code

This only has code for starting, opening and closing files, and for exiting from the program – everything else is written into the child form.

New and **Open** are written directly into their menu items' Click event handlers. The close routine is handled in a separate sub, so that the code can be used by both the **Close** and **Exit** menu items.

```
Public Class Form1
   Inherits System.Windows.Forms.Form

# Windows Form Designer generated code
 Private Sub FileNewChild_Click(ByVal sender As System.Object, ByVal
e As System.EventArgs) Handles FileNewChild.Click
 Dim NewChild As New ChildForm        ' declare the form variable
 NewChild.MdiParent = Me              ' set the parent form
 NewChild.Show()                      ' display the new form
End Sub

 Private Sub FileOpen_Click(ByVal sender As System.Object, ByVal e
As System.EventArgs) Handles FileOpen.Click
 OpenFileDialog1.Filter = "Rich Text Format|*.rtf"
 If OpenFileDialog1.ShowDialog() = DialogResult.OK Then
  Dim NewChild As New ChildForm       ' create a new child
  NewChild.MdiParent = Me             ' load the file into the child
  NewChild.Workspace.LoadFile(OpenFileDialog1.FileName)
  NewChild.Text = OpenFileDialog1.FileName
  NewChild.Show()
 End If
End Sub

 Private Sub FileCloseChild_Click(ByVal sender As System.Object,
ByVal e As System.EventArgs) Handles FileCloseChild.Click
```

```
    CloseChild()
End Sub

Private Sub CloseChild()
  Dim activeChild As Form = Me.ActiveMdiChild
  If activeChild Is Nothing Then Exit Sub
  activeChild.Close()              ' close the window
  activeChild.Dispose()            ' reclaim the memory
End Sub

  Private Sub FileExit_Click(ByVal sender As System.Object, ByVal e
As System.EventArgs) Handles FileExit.Click
  ' close every child window
  While Not (Me.ActiveMdiChild Is Nothing)
   CloseChild()
  End While
  End
End Sub

End Class
```

The Child code

Much of this code is based on the single-window text editor that we developed in Chapter 7 – and some intelligent cut-and-paste could save you quite a bit of typing.

```
Public Class ChildForm
  Inherits  System.Windows.Forms.Form
  Dim saved As Boolean
  Dim MyFileName As String = ""

# Windows Form Designer generated code

Private Sub FileSave_Click(ByVal sender As System.Object, ByVal  e
As System.EventArgs) Handles FileSave.Click
  If MyFileName <> "" Then
   Workspace.SaveFile(MyFileName)   ' resave current file
   saved = True
  Else
   SaveAs()                         ' go to the Save dialog box
  End If
End Sub

Private Sub FileSaveAs_Click(ByVal sender As Object, ByVal e As
System.EventArgs) Handles FileSaveAs.Click
  SaveAs()
End Sub

Private Sub SaveAs()
  SaveFileDialog1.Filter = "Rich Text Format|*.rtf"
```

```
    SaveFileDialog1.Title = "Save document"
   If SaveFileDialog1.ShowDialog() = DialogResult.OK Then
    Workspace.SaveFile(SaveFileDialog1.FileName)
    MyFileName = SaveFileDialog1.FileName
    Me.Text = MyFileName
    saved = True
   End If
 End Sub

 Private Sub CheckSave()
  Dim saveNow As Short
  If Not saved Then
   saveNow = MsgBox("Save the document?", 3, "Save file?")
   If saveNow = 6 Then SaveAs()
  End If
 End Sub
   Private Sub EditCut_Click(ByVal sender As Object, ByVal e As
 System.EventArgs) Handles EditCut.Click
  Clipboard.SetDataObject(Workspace.SelectedText)
  Workspace.SelectedText = ""
 End Sub
   Private Sub EditCopy_Click(ByVal sender As System.Object, ByVal e
 As System.EventArgs) Handles EditCopy.Click
  Clipboard.SetDataObject(Workspace.SelectedText)
 End Sub
   Private Sub EditPaste_Click(ByVal sender As Object, ByVal e As
 System.EventArgs) Handles EditPaste.Click
  Dim data As IDataObject = Clipboard.GetDataObject()
  If data.GetDataPresent(DataFormats.Text) Then
   Workspace.SelectedText = data.GetData(DataFormats.Text)
  End If
 End Sub
   Private Sub WindowCascade_Click(ByVal sender As System.Object, ByVal
 e As System.EventArgs) Handles WindowCascade.Click
  Me.ParentForm.LayoutMdi(MdiLayout.Cascade)
 End Sub
   Private Sub WindowTileHorizontal_Click(ByVal sender As Object, ByVal
 e As System.EventArgs) Handles WindowTileHorizontal.Click
  Me.ParentForm.LayoutMdi(MdiLayout.TileHorizontal)
 End Sub
   Private Sub WindowTileVertical_Click(ByVal sender As Object, ByVale
 As System.EventArgs) Handles WindowTileVertical.Click
  Me.ParentForm.LayoutMdi(MdiLayout.TileVertical)
 End Sub
```

```
    Private Sub Workspace_TextChanged(ByVal sender As System.Object, ByVal
e As System.EventArgs) Handles Workspace. TextChanged
    saved = False
End Sub

Private Sub ChildForm_Closed(ByVal sender As Object, ByVal e As
System.EventArgs) Handles MyBase.Closed
CheckSave()
End Sub

    Private Sub ChildForm_Load(ByVal sender As Object, ByVal e As
System.EventArgs) Handles MyBase.Load
    ' if window was started by Open, the filename is in the title bar
    If Me.Text <> "Document" Then MyFileName = Me.Text
End Sub

End Class
```

10.9 Exercises

10.1 Add a third form to the MDI demo. This one should contain a PictureBox with the Dock property set to Fill. Adapt the code so that it can either load RTF files into the RichTextBox form or image files (*.bmp, *.jpg, *.pcx or *.gif) into the new form.

10.2 Starting from scratch, create an MDI version of the image viewer.

11 Sequential files

We have already seen how TextBoxes, and some other objects, have their own methods for writing their data to and reading it from files. Here we look at how variables and other data can be written to file.

11.1 Saving data to file

Visual Basic can handle both sequential and random access files.

- A **sequential** file has no particular structure, but consists of a set of data items – of the same or different types – stored in the order in which they were written to the disk. To make sense of the data in the file, it must be read back in the right order, into the right type of variables.

  Sequential files are typically used where there is a mixture of information to be stored, or for permanent storage of data that is held in an array during program run-time. Data files created by word-processors or spreadsheets are often be stored as sequential files.

- A **random access** file will hold a set of records, each with an identical structure and at an identifiable place in the file. If a record's position is known, it can be read directly from the file, edited and returned to the same place.

  Database management programs normally hold their data in random access files, though if the whole database will fit in memory a viable alternative is to hold the data in an array and store it on disk as a sequential file.

Using a sequential file

Within a program, files are accessed through a file number. The link between the external (disk) filename and the internal file number is made through the `FileOpen()` method. Its syntax takes the form:

```
FileOpen(filenumber, filename, Openmode.option)
```

The *filenumber* can be given directly. It is usually safe to number the first file you open as 1. If further files are opened while this is still in use, they can then be numbered 2, 3 and so on.

The *filename* is a string expression or variable.

The Openmode *options* are:

Append, to add data to the end of an existing file;
Binary, to open a file for binary access;
Input, to read from an existing file;
Output, to create a new file, replacing any of the same name;
Random, to open a file for random access (see Chapter 12).

FreeFile

There is a possibility that your file numbers may coincide with others used by other applications in the computer. If you prefer to be sure that there will be no conflict with an existing open file, you can get the number of the next free file handle with the `FreeFile()` function, using the line:

```
filenum = FreeFile()
```

At the end of the filing session, the link is ended with the Close statement that ensures that all data is written safely to disk. It takes the form:

```
FileClose(filenumber)
```

Writing and reading data

Once the file has been opened, data can be written to it with these commands:

```
Print (filenumber, item, item, ...)

PrintLine (filenumber, item, item, ...)

Write (filenumber, item, item, ...)

WriteLine (filenumber, item, item, ...)
```

In all cases, there can be any number of items, separated by commas, and they can be any mixture of variables, literal values or functions – in fact, any text that can be printed on screen or paper can be written to a file.

Print() and PrintLine()

The `Print()` method is designed for use when you are creating files that will later be sent to the printer, e.g. reports from a database. With Print, the dates, numbers and currency are formatted using the regional settings in Windows on the PC.

    `PrintLine()` is the same, except that the carriage return and newline characters (Chr(13) and Chr(10)) are sent after the last item.

    If there is any possibility that you may later need to read data back from a Printed file, strings will need special handling. Any that contain commas or newline characters, should be enclosed in quotes for reasons that will be clear in a moment.

Write() and WriteLine()

The `Write()` method is the one you should normally use when creating data files to be read by your Basic programs – or by any other database systems. It writes data in the standard comma-separated values format. Numbers and dates are written in their simplest forms, strings are enclosed in quotes and items are separated by commas. In the WriteLine() variation, the carriage return and newline characters are sent after the data.

Input()

Data is read back from the file with:

```
Input(filenumber, variable)
```

The *variable* must be of the right type. If the file has a succession of different types of data, you will therefore need a matching series of Input()s to read in each item. (Anything could be read into a string variable, but you would probably then need code to convert it into its proper type, and smaller numbers can be read by bigger number variables.) Prove it to yourself with this demo – it writes four items of different data types to file, then reads them back. Type it into a Button's Click sub.

```
Private Sub Button1_Click(ByVal sender As System.Object, ByVal e As
System.EventArgs) Handles Button1.Click
    Dim ShortNum As Short
    Dim myDate As Date
    Dim bigNum As Double
    Dim myBool As Boolean

    FileOpen(1, "testfile", OpenMode.Output)
    Write(1, 7, CDate("17/05/04"), 123456.789, True)
    ' writes Short, Date, Double and Boolean data items
    FileClose(1)
    FileOpen(1, "testfile", OpenMode.Input)
    Input(1, ShortNum)
    MsgBox(ShortNum)
    Input(1, myDate)
    MsgBox(myDate)
    Input(1, bigNum)
    MsgBox(bigNum)
    Input(1, myBool)
    MsgBox(myBool)
    FileClose(1)
End Sub
```

Build and run this. When you click the Button, you should see a succession of four MsgBoxes showing the date items. Now return to the code and move the Input and MsgBox lines for ShortNum to the end of the set. Build, run and try it again. What happens?

Type the following into a Button's Click procedure to see the difference between `Write()` and `Print()` in the way they handle strings and commas. It writes a phrase to disk, closes the file, then reopens it, reads the text back in and prints it on the form.

```
    Private Sub WriteBtn_Click(ByVal sender As System.Object, ByVal e As
System.EventArgs) Handles Writebtn.Click
    Dim phrase, instring As String
    FileOpen(1, "Dolittle", OpenMode.Output)
    phrase = "The rain in Spain, and elsewhere in Iberia, falls mainly on
the plain"
    Write(1, phrase)
    FileClose(1)

    FileOpen(1, "Dolittle", OpenMode.Input)
    Input(1, instring)
    MsgBox(instring)
    FileClose(1)
End Sub
```

Click on the form and you should see "The rain in Spain, and elsewhere in Iberia, falls mainly on the plain".

Now replace `Write(1, phrase)` with `Print(1, phrase)`. Run the program again. This time, you should see only "The rain in Spain". `Input()` spotted the comma and assumed that it marked the end of the string. If there was a second Input() at this point, it would collect "and elsewhere in Iberia".

If you are using Print() to write strings to files, any text containing commas must be explicitly enclosed in quotes. It is often easiest to do this via the ASCII code, as Chr(34). Try it again, this time with the `Print()` line rewritten like this:

```
    Print(1, Chr(34) & phrase & chr(34))
```

11.2 Basic filing

This next simple example shows some of the key concepts of handling sequential files. It writes data to a file, reads it back and removes the file from the disk. The file has been named "temp.$$$", which should be sufficiently unusual not to conflict with any files you have already.

To implement it, place three Buttons on a new form, and name them *ReadBtn*, *WriteBtn* and *DelBtn*. There are only three subs, each attached to the appropriate Button.

The first, **Write**, creates a telephone contacts list by taking in a series of names and phone numbers and writing them to disk.

```
    Private Sub WriteBtn_Click(ByVal sender As System.Object, ByVal e As
System.EventArgs) Handles WriteBtn.Click
    Dim person, telno As String
    FileOpen(1, "temp.$$$", OpenMode.Output)
    Do
        person = InputBox("Name of contact or Enter to stop")
        If person = "" Then Exit Do
```

```
        telno = InputBox("Tel no")
        Write(1, person, telno)
    Loop
    FileClose(1)
End Sub
```

The second, **Read**, inputs the data from the file and prints it on the screen. You will see that the data is read in the same order in which it was written. Try inputting the data the other way round and see what happens.

Notice the test used on the Loop – **Until EOF(1)**. **EOF** is End Of File. This function picks up the code that signals the end of the disk file.

```
Private Sub ReadBtn_Click(ByVal sender As System.Object, ByVal e As
System.EventArgs) Handles ReadBtn.Click
    Dim person, telno As String
    FileOpen(1, "temp.$$$", OpenMode.Input)
    Do
        Input(1, person)
        Input(1, telno)
        MsgBox(person & " Tel: " & telno)
    Loop Until EOF(1)
    FileClose(1)
End Sub
```

The last, **Remove**, is simply there for tidying purposes – it deletes the file from the disk using the `Kill()` method.

```
Private Sub DelBtn_Click(ByVal sender As System.Object, ByVal e As
System.EventArgs) Handles DelBtn.Click
    Kill("temp.$$$")
End Sub
```

Kill with care! It really does delete files – they are not passed to the Recycle Bin in Windows, and cannot be recovered.

Task 11.1

Implement the Read and Write program and test it with a variety of data. What difference would it make if the *telno* variable was an Integer?

11.3 Data analysis and storage

This demonstration program performs simple statistical analysis on sets of data, and allows sets to be saved to and loaded in from disk. The analysis is limited to giving the maximum, minimum, total and mean values. All are produced and displayed together. If you wrote the data analysis program set as an exercise in Chapter 4, you could use that as the base of this example. There are five procedures in the program, run from a simple menu.

```
        &File              &Data
            &Write             &Create
            &Read              &Analyse
            E&xit
```

The form is empty apart from the menu and one textbox, with its Multiline property set to true.

The code

The data sets can be of any size as the dimension of the *data* array is determined by the user when creating each new set. The undimensioned array is set up at the global level, along with a *count* variable which will be used to store the size.

```
Public Class Form1
    Inherits System.Windows.Forms.Form
    Dim data() As Single              ' undimensioned array
    Dim count As Integer = 0
```

The **Create** routine starts by asking the user for the number of elements in the set, then dimensions the array with the ReDim statement. Note that the loop then runs from 0 to *count* – 1, to match the subscripts fo the new array. The data values are collected through an InputBox, as it provides the simplest method of getting values.

```
    Private Sub DataCreate_Click(ByVal sender As System.Object, ByVal e
As System.EventArgs) Handles DataCreate.Click
    count = InputBox("How many elements?")
    ReDim data(count)
    Dim element As Integer
    For element = 0 To count - 1
       data(element) = InputBox("Entry value for element no " & element)
    Next
End Sub
```

Ideally, there should be another routine to edit or add data to the set, but I'm trying to keep things simple. Your users will just have to get it right first time!

The **Analysis** should be self-explanatory, as it uses standard routines to find the total, average, maximum and minimum values in the data set. You might note the use of the constant *vbCrLf* which holds characters 13 and 10 (carriage return and line feed). These allow the outputs to be written on four separate lines.

```
    Private Sub DataAnalyse_Click(ByVal sender As System.Object, ByVal e
As System.EventArgs) Handles DataAnalyse.Click
    Dim total, average, max, min As Single
    Dim n As Integer
    max = data(0)
    min = data(0)
    For n = 1 To count - 1
       If data(n) > max Then max = data(n)
```

```
         If data(n) < min Then min = data(n)
         total += data(n)
      Next
      average = total / count
      Display.Text = "Total = " & total & vbCrLf
      Display.Text &= "Average = " & average & vbCrLf
      Display.Text &= "Max value = " & max & vbCrLf
      Display.Text &= "Min value = " & min & vbCrLf
   End Sub
```

The **Write** routine uses an InputBox to get a filename – a crude but effective approach which you may prefer to replace with one that uses the SaveFileDialog.

When we write the data to file, we must think ahead to what will happen when it is read back in. The array will have to be ReDimensioned for the incoming data, which means that the program will need to know the size of the array before it starts to read its data. The solution is to write MaxNumber as the first value on the file.

```
   Private Sub FileWrite_Click(ByVal sender As System.Object, ByVal e As
System.EventArgs) Handles FileWrite.Click
      Dim n As Integer
      Dim fname As String
      Dim fnum As Integer
      fname = InputBox("Name of file")
      fnum = FreeFile()
      FileOpen(fnum, fname, OpenMode.Output)
      Write(1, count)
      For n = 0 To count - 1
         WriteLine(1, data(n))
      Next
      FileClose(fnum)
   End Sub
```

Figure 11.1

The data has been analysed and is about to be written to file

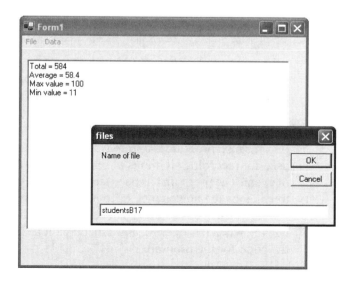

The **Read** code can be created by copying and editing the Write routine, as the two can be very similar. You will need to add the `ReDim` line, and replace `OpenMode.Output` and `Write()` by `OpenMode.Input` and `Input()`.

```
Private Sub FileRead_Click(ByVal sender As System.Object, ByVal e As
System.EventArgs) Handles FileRead.Click
   Dim n As Integer
   Dim fname As String
   Dim fnum As Integer
   fname = InputBox("Name of file")
   fnum = FreeFile()
   FileOpen(fnum, fname, OpenMode.Input)
   Input(fnum, count)
   ReDim data(count)
   For n = 1 To count
      Input(1, data(n))
   Next
   FileClose(fnum)
End Sub
```

The `For` loop handles the Input well here, as we know the number of items to be read. As we saw in the last example, where there is an unknown quantity of data on the file, we can use a loop that checks for the End Of File, with the EOF function.

Task 11.2

Take the simple data analysis program that you developed earlier and add these new subs to it. Test each new sub as it is added, and test the whole program thoroughly when it is complete. What additional features or error-traps does it need?

11.4 Appending to files

When you open a file for writing in Output mode, the data will overwrite anything that may be there already. This is what you want if the data is stored in an array during editing and process, but sometimes you want to keep the existing filed data intact, and add new data to the end of the file. For this you need to open the file in Append mode.

This next program is a simple demonstration of this approach. Here, the files are used for recording sightings of birds, but they could be used for logging any types of event. The program has been stripped down to a minimum, so if you feel the need to enhance the appearance or to add facilities or error-trapping, please do so!

The form needs a Label, named *Display*, which is used for showing the contents of a log when it is opened, and a menu with five entries. We can use these to outline the code for the program.

Menu item Operations

New log   Get the filename
Open the file in Output mode.

Open log   Get the filename
Open the file in Input mode
Input and display the contents
Close the file
Open the file again in Append mode

Add entry Check that a file is open
Get the data for the event and write to file

Close log Close the file

Exit   End.

The **Open log** routine could be simplified by taking out the input and display lines
– display could be hived off into a separate sub.

Here's the full code.

```
Public Class Form1
   Inherits System.Windows.Forms.Form
   Dim logname As String = ""
   Dim filenum As Integer


Windows Form Designer generated code


   Private Sub NewLog_Click(ByVal sender As System.Object, ByVal e As
System.EventArgs) Handles NewLog.Click
   logname = InputBox("Name for new log?")
   filenum = FreeFile()
   FileOpen(filenum, logname, OpenMode.Output)
   Display.Text = ""
End Sub

Private Sub OpenLog_Click(ByVal sender As System.Object, ByVal e As
System.EventArgs) Handles OpenLog.Click
   Dim entryDate As Date
   Dim num As Short
   Dim sighting As String

   logname = InputBox("Name of log?")
   filenum = FreeFile()
   FileOpen(filenum, logname, OpenMode.Input)
   Display.Text = "Date        Number    Sighting" & vbCrLf
   Do
      Input(filenum, entryDate)
      Input(filenum, num)
      Input(filenum, sighting)
```

```
         Display.Text &= entryDate & " " & num & "   " & sighting & vbCrLf
      Loop Until EOF(filenum)
      FileClose(filenum)
      FileOpen(filenum, logname, OpenMode.Append)
   End Sub
   Private Sub AddEntry_Click(ByVal sender As System.Object, ByVal e As
System.EventArgs) Handles AddEntry.Click
      Dim entryDate As Date
      Dim num As Short
      Dim sighting As String

      If logname = "" Then
         MsgBox("No log open")
         Exit Sub
      End If
      entryDate = CDate(InputBox("Date of sighting"))
      num = CShort(InputBox("Number seen"))
      sighting = InputBox("Type of bird")
      WriteLine(1, entryDate, num, sighting)
   End Sub
   Private Sub CloseLog_Click(ByVal sender As System.Object, ByVal e As
System.EventArgs) Handles CloseLog.Click
      FileClose(filenum)
      Display.Text = ""
   End Sub
   Private Sub FileExit_Click(ByVal sender As System.Object, ByVal e As
System.EventArgs) Handles FileExit.Click
      End
   End Sub
End Class
```

Figure 11.2

Composite screenshots showing the data entry InputBox against the display of an existing file

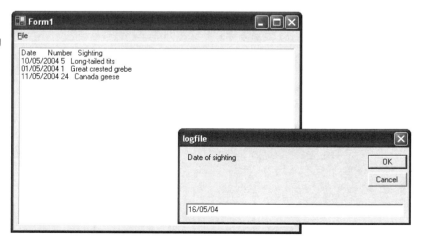

11.5 Worked example: Hangman

This next example brings together the string manipulation and graphics management of Chapter 7 and 8, with the file-handling techniques covered here, to produce an implementation of the old favourite word game.

Handling hangman's files

The program draws on a text file – the word list – and a set of image files. These are all loaded automatically, as needed, so the code must set the paths and the filenames to open the files. The program assumes that the text and image files are all stored in the same folder, and its location is stored in the variable *myPath*. In the example, this is defined as "C:\vb\hangman" – replace this with the right path for your files.

To get a word at the start of a new game, the program opens the file of words, assembling the filename from the path and name:

```
wordfile = myPath & "\words.txt"
FileOpen(Fnum, wordfile, OpenMode.Input)
```

It then reads from the file a random number of times. (I have 26 words in my file, from 'Aardvark' to 'Zebra' – set your random number limits to suit your word list.)

```
times = Rnd() * 26
For n = 1 To times
    Input(Fnum, target)
Next n
```

As we will be opening the file again for the next word, it is important to close it after we have finished inputting.

```
FileClose(Fnum)
```

Figure 11.3

A possible layout for the hangman form, with the active controls labelled.

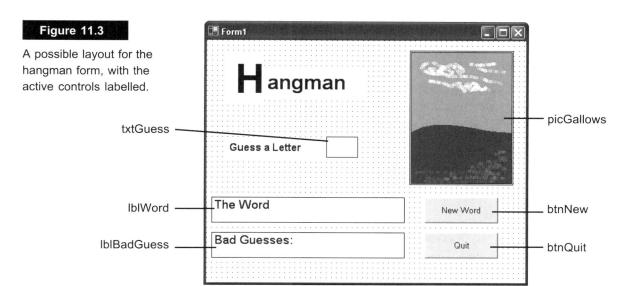

Loading image files is basically simpler – though the command line is a bit heavy! As part of the New routine, the blank background image (*"hang0.bmp"*) is loaded.

```
picGallows.Image = System.Drawing.Image.FromFile(myPath & "\hang0.bmp")
```

It gets a little more complicated when we are loading the images that gradually build the gallows. These are named *"hang1.bmp"* to *"hang10.bmp"*. This lines create the filename by joing the start and end parts with the number, held in *PicNo*.

```
picname = myPath & "\hang" & PicNo & ".bmp"
```

The image can then be loaded using the same `FromFile()` method as above.

String him up

String manipulation is at the heart of this word games. Let's look at how it works. The word is loaded into *target*. It is converted into uppercase – as the guessed letters are during the game – then copied into *workCopy*. During the course of the game, the letters in *target* will be overwritten as they are guessed, so we must keep an intact copy for checking against.

```
target = UCase(target)
workCopy = target
```

If we were playing on paper, we would write a set of dashes that letters would be written on as they were guessed. On a computer, a set of dashes can blur into one long line, so I've used asterisks instead as placeholders for the unknown letters.

Notice how the `New String(...)` expression can be used to create a string composed of a number of the same characters:

```
letters = Len(target)
lblWord.Text = New String("*", letters)
```

The guess-checking routine is written into the TextChange event of *txtGuess*, so that it is activated as soon as someone enters a letter. The letter is converted to uppercase and stored in *guess*. The code then loops through the letters in target, comparing *guess* with each in turn

```
For n = 1 To Len(target)
    If guess = Mid(target, n, 1) Then
```

If they match, the guessed letter is written into *lblWord*'s asterisks at the appropriate point, and *target*'s letter is overwritten with an asterisk.

```
Mid(lblWord.Text, n, 1) = guess
Mid(target, n, 1) = "*"
```

Writing into *lblWord* triggers its TextChange event. We can put a test here to see if the word has been fully guessed.

```
If lblWord.Text = workCopy Then MsgBox("You Win")
```

That's the core of the checking, though the actual routine has a little bit more to it. The Boolean variable *inword* is set to False at the start, and to True if a match is found. This is then used to control the next part of the code, which adds the latter to the 'Bad Guesses:' list and draws the next part of the gallows.

Hangman: the code

Here's the full code for the game. It assumes that you have a form set up with the named controls shown in Figure 11.3, and that you have a set of files named *hang0.bmp* through to *hang10.bmp*, which progressively draw the gallows and hanged man. (And this is a children's game!)

```vb
Public Class Form1
   Inherits System.Windows.Forms.Form
Windows Form Designer generated code
   Dim target As String
   Dim workCopy As String
   Dim guesses As Short
   Dim found As Short
   Dim PicNo As Short
   Dim myPath As String
   Private Sub Form1_Load(ByVal eventSender As System.Object, ByVal
eventArgs As System.EventArgs) Handles MyBase.Load
   myPath = "C:\vb\hangman"            ' or wherever your files are
   Randomize()                        ' ensure new random sequence
   newgame()
End Sub
   Private Sub btnNew_Click(ByVal eventSender As System.Object, ByVal
eventArgs As System.EventArgs) Handles btnNew.Click
   newgame()
End Sub
Private Sub newgame()
   Dim letters As String
   Dim n As Short
   Dim times As Short
   Dim wordfile As String
   Dim Fnum As Short
   Fnum = FreeFile()
   wordfile = myPath & "\words.txt"           ' or wherever/whatever
   FileOpen(Fnum, wordfile, OpenMode.Input)
   times = Rnd() * 26
   For n = 1 To times
      Input(Fnum, target)
   Next n
   FileClose(Fnum)
   target = UCase(target)
   workCopy = target
   letters = Len(target)                      ' how many letters?
   lblWord.Text = New String("*", letters)
   guesses = 0
```

```
      found = 0
      lblBadGuess.Text = "Bad Guesses: "
      picGallows.Image = System.Drawing.Image.FromFile(myPath & "\hang0.bmp")
      PicNo = 1
End Sub
   Private Sub txtGuess_TextChanged(ByVal eventSender As System.Object,
ByVal eventArgs As System.EventArgs) Handles txtGuess.TextChanged
      Dim picname As String
      Dim temp As String
      Dim n As Short
      Dim inword As Boolean
      Dim guess As String
      If txtGuess.Text = "" Then Exit Sub        ' when box is cleared
      guess = UCase(txtGuess.Text)
      If guess < "A" Or guess > "Z" Then txtGuess.Text = "" : Exit Sub
      'check word
      inword = False
      For n = 1 To Len(target)
         If guess = Mid(target, n, 1) Then
            inword = True
            Mid(temp, n, 1) = guess          ' write it into the word
            Mid(target, n, 1) = "*"           ' mark it off
            found = found + 1
         End If
      Next n
      If Not inword Then
         lblBadGuess.Text &= & guess
         picname = myPath & "\hang" & PicNo & ".bmp"
         picGallows.Image = System.Drawing.Image.FromFile(picname)
         PicNo += 1
         If PicNo = 11 Then MsgBox("The word was " & workCopy)
      End If
      txtGuess.Text = ""
End Sub
   Private Sub lblWord_TextChanged(ByVal sender As Object, ByVal e As
System.EventArgs) Handles lblWord.TextChanged
      If lblWord.Text = workCopy Then MsgBox("You Win")
End Sub
   Private Sub btnQuit_Click(ByVal eventSender As System.Object, ByVal
eventArgs As System.EventArgs) Handles btnQuit.Click
      End
End Sub
End Class
```

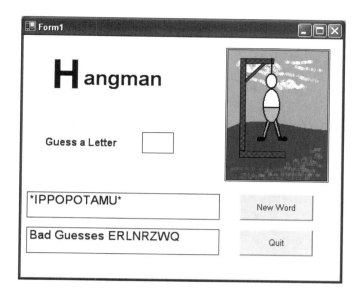

Figure 11.4

Close to the end of a game
– only two lives left and I
haven't a clue what this
animal might be...

11.6 Exercises

11.1 RadioButtons provide a convenient way of handling responses to multiple-choice tests, for their captions can display the alternative answers and only one can be selected. Design and implement a program which will read a file containing questions, answers and the right answer, taking one question at a time and displaying it with a set of option Buttons. The file itself can be created in Write or any word processor that can output an ASCII text file.

11.2 Payroll programs often store their data in sequential files, as every record is accessed at each payrun. Write a program to manage a simplified system. It must have routines to add and remove employees, as well as to calculate and print the weekly payslips. The file should contain the employee's name, reference number, hourly rate, tax code, total earnings for the year to date and total tax paid to date. When calculating the week's pay, assume that the first 37 hours are paid at the normal rate and additional hours at time and a half.

A possible solution to Exercises 11.1 is given in the Appendix. Exercise 11.2 is very open-ended – if the program works, it must be right!

12 Records and random access files

Record structures can be used in many situations where it is useful to keep varied items of data together, but their most prominent use is in association with random access files.

12.1 Record structures

In Visual Basic you can define your own record structures, in the same way that you can with RECORD in Pascal. Of course, being Visual Basic, it gives you far more flexibility and a far wider range of data types than you get with Pascal, but we won't go into the more exotic parts in this introductory book. Record structures are defined by the `Structure` statement, and must be written at the top of a form or a Basic module. Definition takes the form:

```
Structure record_name
   var_name As data_type
   var_name As data_type
   ....
End Structure
```

The definition of the subordinate variables (the *fields*) within the record follows the normal rules for variable declaration, with one significant exception – the lengths of strings must be specified. This gives the records a fixed size, which is needed when allocating space in memory or on disk.

The length is set by writing the `<VBFixedString(length)>` attribute at the start of the definiton line. For example, if you were creating a student database, and wanted to hold the name, phone number, fees, and end-of-year results for each student, the record structure might be defined by:

```
Structure StudentRecord
 <VBFixedString(30)>  FullName As String
 <VBFixedString(12)>  TelNo As String
   Fees As Currency
   Marks(10) As Integer
End Structure
```

This allocates 30 characters for the name and 12 for the phone number – before deciding on these limits, the wise designer would have taken a sample of the data to be stored and found the longest items in each string field. Note that *Marks()* is an array. You can have arrays *within* records and you can have arrays *of* records.

If the structure is declared in a form, variables of its type can only be declared within that form. If you have more than one form and want to have variables of the same structure in different forms, the structure must be defined in a module.

Declaration of variables of the new type, follow the normal pattern.

```
Dim Student As StudentRecord
```

```
Dim Class(30) As StudentRecord
```

The first line sets up a variable to hold the details of one student; the second sets up an array of 01 (0 to 29) record structures.

Within the code, you can treat the whole of the data in a record as a single unit when copying it to another variable of the same type:

```
Class(element) = Student
```

A record can also be written to, and read from, disk by the `FilePut()` and `FileGet()` methods. Both of these handle whole records as units, transferring all the fields in one operation. When you want to input data, or display it, it must be done by individual fields, identifying them by their record variable and field name, separated by a full stop.

```
Display.Text = Student.FullName
```

```
Student.Fees = CCur(InputBox("Enter Fees Paid"))
```

When you are working with arrayed records or arrays within records, the identification can get long-winded:

```
Class(StudentNo).Marks(AssNo) = txtMarks.Text
```

Here we have an array of records called *Class*; *StudentNo* identifies the individual within the class. One of the fields in the record is *Marks*, and *AssNo* holds the number of the assignment.

12.2 Random access files

Opening a file for random access follows the pattern for sequential files, with two significant variations.

- With sequential files you can only read from or write to them at any one time, so they must be opened for Input, Append or Output. Random access files can be read and written at the same time, and are simply opened `Openmode.Random`.

- The second point to note with these, is that the system needs to know the size of the record structure, so that it knows how to organise the disk space. The `Len()` function – which finds the length of strings – will also give the length of the record. So far we have used the `FileOpen()` function with only three parameters – file number, name and OpenMode. It can take another three, setting the access and sharing permissions and the record length. We are not using the fourth and fifth parameters, but their places must be marked by commas.

Typical opening lines for a random access file look like this:

```
recLength = Len(student)

FileOpen(fnum, "student.dat", OpenMode.Random, , recLength)
```

This sets up a link with a file called "student.dat" – creating a new one if there is no matching file there at the time. The size of each record will be the total number of bytes in the *student* type.

FileGet()

Records are read with the `FileGet()` method. It is given the filenumber, the name of the variable into which data is to be copied and the position of the record in the file – if you want to change the position

```
FileGet(Fnum, Student, RecNum)
```

This will copy the data in the file linked to *Fnum*, into the variable *Student* from record number *RecNum*.

You can read the record at the current position with the simpler expression:

```
FileGet(Fnum, Student, )
```

Note that trying to read beyond the end of the file will produce an error.

FilePut()

Writing to the file is handled by the `FilePut()` method, which follows the same pattern.

```
FilePut(Fnum, Student, RecNum)
```

This would replace any existing data at record number *RecNum*, or create a new record at that position.

```
FilePut(Fnum, Student, )
```

This would write at the current position in the file.

Seek()

Positioning in the file can also be handled by the `Seek()` function. This can be used in two ways. It will return the position of the current record, when used like this:

```
RecNum = Seek(Fnum)
```

It can also be used to set the position – give it the record number:

```
Seek(Fnum, RecNum)
```

Then read or write the record at the new (current) position.

```
FileGet(Fnum, Student, )
```

One last function to note, before moving on to an example, is **LOF()**. This returns the Length Of a File, and can be used in conjunction with *Len()* to work out how many records there are in a file:

```
NumberOfRecords = LOF(Fnum) \ Len(Record)
```

12.3 The staff database

Students are often asked to write student database programs. I thought it would make a change to design one to handle the lecturing staff.

With any database program the design must start from the data itself – what do we want to store, and what do we want to get out of it?

The nature of the data

For each member of staff we will hold:

Name	String, 30 characters should be enough
Reference Number	also acts as the record number – Integer
Department	String, 10 characters are enough
Grade	an Integer
Teaching Hours	may contain fractions, so Single

From this we can derive the Structure definition:

```
Structure lecturer
      Dim Refno As Integer
      <VBFixedString(30)> Dim LName As String
      <VBFixedString(10)> Dim Dept As String
      Dim Grade As Integer
      Dim Hours As Single
   End Structure
```

As the data is held on file, and each record can be accessed when wanted, there is no need for any global variables, and only a few, to handle the file itself, are needed at the general level. These are the only ones we need:

```
Dim staff As lecturer             ' record variable
Dim Fnum As Integer               ' filenumber
Dim RecCount As Integer           ' number of records
Dim recLength As Long = Len(staff)  ' length of a record
Dim allrecs As Boolean            ' needed by print routines
```

This gives us a record variable called *staff*, with the fields *staff.RefNo*, *staff.LName*, *staff.Dept*, *staff.Grade* and *staff.Hours*.

Processing required

1   Enter data and keep the records up to date. We therefore need routines to add, delete and edit records. If TextBoxes are used to collect (and display) data, their built-in editing facilities will do away with the need for a special edit routine.

New and edited records should be saved before they are removed from the screen. We can do this by writing a save operation at the start of all routines that change the record on display.

2 We need to be able to display the details of any individual and of all lecturers.

The main data entry/display shows one record, and will need routines that will step forwards and backwards through the records.

To show all the records, we could use a multi-line TextBox. This could be on a second form, or on the same form but hidden away when not needed. I've used the latter approach (we looked at multiple form programs in Chapter 10).

3 We need to be able to print details of one or all lecturers, so a PrintDocument control must be added to the form.

4 We want to be able to find any individual, searching either by name or reference number.

5 We want to be able to select groups, based on either their department or grade.

The operations can be translated to a set of commands and a menu structure:

File	Record	Query
View All Records	Add	Find
Print	Delete	By Name
This Record	Next	By Number
Print All Records	Previous	Select
Exit		By Department
		By Grade

In a program like this, where each procedure stands largely by itself, linked to others only through the common data file, it is simplest to discuss the design and coding of each separately.

Figure 12.1

The staff database form.

The Visible property of *Display* and *CloseBtn* should be set to False.

Use **Format > Order > Send to Front** to set *Display* at the front when all the other controls are in place.

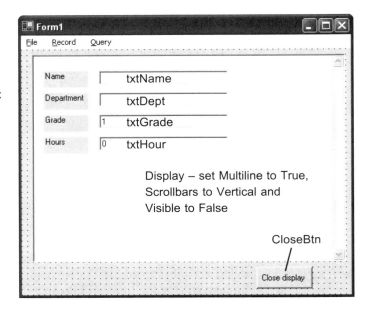

12.4 Initialisation and data entry/edit

Initialisation

This is best done in the `Form Load` procedure, which will be executed as soon as the program starts. Initialisation operations are:

```
open the connection to the data file;
find out how many records there are on disk;
pick up the first one;
if the file is being accessed for the first time,
   allocate a reference number for the first record;
display the record on screen
```

As we will want an identical display routine at several points in the program, it makes sense to set this up as a separate procedure. Here's the initialisation code:

```
Private Sub Form1_Load(ByVal sender As System.Object, ByVal e As
System.EventArgs) Handles MyBase.Load
  Fnum = FreeFile()
  FileOpen(Fnum, "Staff.dta", OpenMode.Random, , , recLength)
  RecCount = LOF(Fnum) / reclength
  ' open at first record - if any
  If RecCount > 0 Then
    FileGet(Fnum, staff, 1)
  Else
    staff.Refno = 1
    RecCount = 1
  End If
  showrec()
End Sub
```

The *showrec* procedure is designed to work on the current record, so that must be selected and its data read before calling this procedure. It will copy the fields into the appropriate TextBoxes on the Form. The reference number must not be open to change, so should be written into a Label or combined with a little heading text and made into the Form's Text, to appear in the title bar.

```
Private Sub showrec()
  Me.Text = "Staff Database Rec No: " & staff.Refno
  txtName.Text = staff.LName
  txtDept.Text = staff.Dept
  txtGrade.Text = staff.Grade
  txtHours.Text = staff.Hours
End Sub
```

Display and Edit Controls

The `TextChange` event of the TextBoxes can be used to pick up any changes made to the displayed data. Values can then be copied to the record – after processing.

- The *Grade* and *Hours* must be converted to numeric values before passing to the record's fields, or there will be a 'Wrong data type' error.
- The *Name* and *Dept* could be copied straight to the fields, but it is best to remove any leading spaces first, using the `Trim()` function. Spaces can creep in and may complicate search operations.

```
Private Sub txtName_TextChanged(ByVal sender As System.Object, ByVal
e As System.EventArgs) Handles txtName.TextChanged
   staff.LName = Trim(txtName.Text)
End Sub

   Private Sub txtDept_TextChanged(ByVal sender As System.Object, ByVal
e As System.EventArgs) Handles txtDept.TextChanged
   staff.Dept = Trim(txtDept.Text)
End Sub

   Private Sub txtGrade_TextChanged(ByVal sender As System.Object,
ByVal e As System.EventArgs) Handles txtGrade.TextChanged
   staff.Grade = Val(txtGrade.Text)
End Sub

   Private Sub txtHours_TextChanged(ByVal sender As System.Object,
ByVal e As System.EventArgs) Handles txtHours.TextChanged
   staff.Hours = Val(txtHours.Text)
End Sub
```

12.5 Record menu options

The *Add*, *Next* and *Previous* procedures will all start by writing the current record to disk, so that any changes made to the current record are stored before another record is read in or created. (To guarantee that all data is always retained, we should write the same `FilePut` line into the start of *all* procedures.)

Add

This procedure must set up a new record, by allocating a reference/record number and clearing the *staff* variable of the current values. The current record is saved at the start, in case there have been any changes.

The reference number is found by adding one to the record count, so the new record always goes at the end of the file.

```
Private Sub RecAdd_Click(ByVal sender As System.Object, ByVal e As
System.EventArgs) Handles RecAdd.Click
   FilePut(Fnum, staff, staff.Refno)    ' write current record to disk
   RecCount = RecCount + 1               ' one more record
   staff.Refno = RecCount                ' create its reference number
   staff.LName = ""                      ' clear out old data
   staff.Dept = ""
```

```
    staff.Grade = 0
    staff.Hours = 0
    showrec()
End Sub
```

Delete

The **Delete** procedure, as implemented here, merely blanks out the data, allowing the reference number to be reused for another person. It does not actually remove the record. The 'Deleted' records are marked by "Blank" in the *Lname* field. A check for this in the Print procedure stops such records from being displayed. The person maintaining the database could look for a Blank record, and overwrite that, when entering the new details for a new member of staff.

```
    Private Sub RecDelete_Click(ByVal sender As System.Object, ByVal e
As System.EventArgs) Handles RecDelete.Click
    staff.LName = "Blank"
    staff.Dept = ""
    staff.Grade = 0
    staff.Hours = 0
    FilePut(Fnum, staff, staff.Refno)
    showrec()
End Sub
```

Gaps in random access files

Visual Basic offers no simple way to delete a record from a random access disk file. We could close up the gaps left by deletions by reading in all the records one at a time, writing valid ones to a new file and replacing the old file with the new, slimmer version. As this changes the reference numbers, it is not a perfect solution, but you may like to write a CleanFile routine that would do this. For more efficient random access file handling, you really have to start indexing them, but that is beyond the scope of this book.

Next

In the **Next** procedure, we can use the `Seek()` function to move on to the next record, checking that there is one before attempting to display it, and giving a 'No More Records' message at the end of the file.

```
    Private Sub RecNext_Click(ByVal sender As System.Object, ByVal e As
System.EventArgs) Handles RecNext.Click
    Dim temp As Integer
    FilePut(Fnum, staff, staff.Refno)        ' store current record
    temp = Seek(Fnum)                        ' find the next
        If temp <= RecCount Then             ' check for the end
```

```
      FileGet(Fnum, staff, temp)
   Else
      MsgBox("No More Records ", 64)
   End If
   showrec()
End Sub
```

Previous

With the **Previous** procedure, we cannot Seek backwards, but we can use the current record's reference number to calculate the position of the previous record. Here we must look for the start of the file, and avoid stepping backwards into oblivion.

```
Private Sub RecPrevious_Click(ByVal sender As System.Object, ByVal e
As System.EventArgs) Handles RecPrevious.Click
   Dim temp As Long
   FilePut(Fnum, staff, staff.Refno)        ' store current record
   temp = staff.Refno - 1                    ' find previous number
   If temp > 0 Then                          ' check for the beginning
      FileGet(Fnum, staff, temp)
   Else
      MsgBox("Start of File ", 64)
   End If
   showrec()
End Sub
```

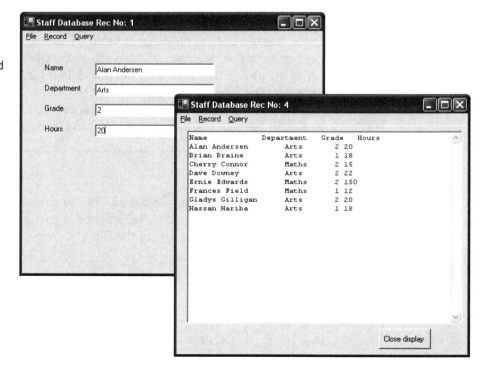

Figure 12.2

The single record and all records displays

12.6 File menu options

View All

The **View All** routine will bring the multi-line TextBox *Display* into view and print headings and the details of all records on it. It is controlled by the *Close Display* Button which has code to make the Textbox (and the Button) invisible again when the user has finished viewing.

This code will give you a reasonably neat layout, but only if you use a monospaced font – one where all characters have the same width, such as Courier. You will need to count spaces carefully (or keep fiddling with them until they are right) to get the headings and the records in line.

Notice the line that checks for deleted records. The simple test:

```
staff.Lname = "Blank"
```

will not do the job, as Lname is a 30 character string. You can either pad out with "Blank   " with 25 spaces, or trim Lname down to its first five.

```
        If Mid(staff.Lname, 1, 5) <> "Blank" Then
```

Here's the whole code:

```
    Private Sub ViewAll_Click(ByVal sender As System.Object, ByVal e As
System.EventArgs) Handles ViewAll.Click
    Dim n As Integer
    Display.Visible = True       ' show the Display TextBox
    CloseBtn.Visible = True      ' and its control button
    Display.Text = "Name           Department   Grade Hours" & vbCrLf
    For n = 1 To RecCount
       FileGet(Fnum, staff, n)
       If Mid(staff.Lname, 1, 5) <> "Blank" Then
          Display.Text &= staff.LName & " " & staff.Dept & " " &
staff.Grade & "    " & staff.Hours & vbCrLf
       End If
    Next n
End Sub
```

The *CloseBtn* Button simply tucks away the Display TextBox and itself.

```
    Private Sub CloseBtn_Click(ByVal sender As System.Object, ByVal e As
System.EventArgs) Handles CloseBtn.Click
    Display.Visible = False
    CloseBtn.Visible = False
End Sub
```

Print

As there is only one PrintDocument, the code for **Print Current Record** and **Print All Records** is all written in the one PrintPage sub. All that the menu event handlers do is set the *allrecs* variable and call up the `Print()` method.

```
   Private Sub PrintAll_Click(ByVal sender As System.Object, ByVal e As
System.EventArgs) Handles PrintAll.Click
    allrecs = True
    PrintDocument1.Print()
End Sub
   Private Sub PrintThis_Click(ByVal sender As System.Object, ByVal e
As System.EventArgs) Handles PrintThis.Click
    allrecs = False
    PrintDocument1.Print()
End Sub
```

The PrintPage routine is based in the one in Chapter 7, but notice these points:
- After the header has been printed, the code splits into two blocks – one for all records and the other for the current record only.
- The DrawString method has parameters to set the print position. Adding 20 to the y value after each record will space out the lines, and if we write each field with a separate DrawString, we can arrange them into columns.

```
   Private Sub PrintDocument1_PrintPage(ByVal sender As System.Object,
ByVal e As System.Drawing.Printing.PrintPageEventArgs) Handles
PrintDocument1.PrintPage
   Dim myFont As New Font("Garamond", 12)          ' choose your own font
   Dim mybrush As New SolidBrush(Color.Black)
   Dim ypos As Single = 20
   Dim n As Integer

   e.Graphics.DrawString("Name        Department   Grade Hours", myFont,
mybrush, 10, ypos)
   If allrecs Then
     For n = 1 To RecCount - 1
       ypos += 20
       FileGet(Fnum, staff, n)
       If Mid(staff.Lname <> "Blank", 1, 5) Then
         e.Graphics.DrawString(staff.LName, myFont, mybrush, 10, ypos)
         e.Graphics.DrawString(staff.Dept, myFont, mybrush, 200, ypos)
         e.Graphics.DrawString(staff.Grade, myFont, mybrush, 350, ypos)
         e.Graphics.DrawString(staff.Hours, myFont, mybrush, 400, ypos)
       End If
     Next
   Else
   'allrecs is False, printing current record only
     ypos += 20
     e.Graphics.DrawString(staff.LName, myFont, mybrush, 10, ypos)
     e.Graphics.DrawString(staff.Dept, myFont, mybrush, 200, ypos)
     e.Graphics.DrawString(staff.Grade, myFont, mybrush, 350, ypos)
     e.Graphics.DrawString(staff.Hours, myFont, mybrush, 400, ypos)
```

```
      End If
End Sub
```

Exit

When the program is closed down with the **Exit** option, the current record is written
and the file closed to ensure that all data is safely on the disk.

```
Private Sub FileExit_Click(ByVal sender As System.Object, ByVal e As
System.EventArgs) Handles FileExit.Click
   FilePut(Fnum, staff, staff.Refno)    ' save changes to current record
   FileClose(Fnum)
   End
End Sub
```

12.7 Find and Select

Find by Number

This is simply a matter of taking the record's index number, checking that it is valid,
and Seeking to that place on the disk.

InputBox and MsgBox are used to get the target in and a message out. You may
prefer to replace these quick but crude boxes with something more sophisticated,
once you have got the main routines working properly.

```
Private Sub FindIndex_Click(ByVal sender As System.Object, ByVal e
As System.EventArgs) Handles FindIndex.Click
   Dim target As Long
   target = InputBox("Enter Reference Number", "Find")
   If target > 0 And target <= RecCount Then
      Seek(Fnum, target)
      FileGet(Fnum, staff, )
      showrec()
   Else
      MsgBox("Record " & target & " not present ", 48)
   End If
End Sub
```

Find by Name

Finding **By Name**, or by any other value held in a field, is a little more complicated.
We can do it by reading through the file, comparing the target value with that of
each record in turn until a match is found, or the end of the file is reached.

The design can be summarised:

```
set Found to false
get target value
```

```
        loop through file
           if matching value found
              display record
              set Found to true
              exit from the loop
        if found still false at the end
           display Not Found message
```

This translates directly to the code:

```
 Private Sub FindName_Click(ByVal sender As System.Object, ByVal e As
System.EventArgs) Handles FindName.Click
   Dim target As String
   Dim n As Integer
   Dim Found As Boolean = False
   target = InputBox("Enter Target Name", "Find")
   For n = 1 To RecCount
      FileGet(Fnum, staff, n)
      If target = RTrim(staff.LName) Then    ' note the trimming
         showrec()
         Found = True                        ' signal success
         Exit For
      End If
   Next n
   If Not Found Then MsgBox("Record " & target & " not present", 48)
End Sub
```

Select

The two **Select** procedures both follow the same pattern as *Find By Name*, but adjusted to cope with the fact that they are hunting for sets of matching records, rather than an individual one. Instead of stopping when a matching record is found and displaying it, all matching records are printed on the all records display. The *Finds* variable is used here to keep a count of the matches.

First select by *department*.

```
 Private Sub SelectDept_Click(ByVal sender As System.Object, ByVal e
As System.EventArgs) Handles SelectDept.Click
   Dim target As String
   Dim Finds As Integer
   Dim n As Integer
   Display.Visible = True
   CloseBtn.Visible = True
   Finds = 0
   target = InputBox("Which Department", "Select")
   Display.Text = "Department: " & target & vbCrLf
   Display.Text = "Name              Grade Hours" & vbCrLf
```

```
      For n = 1 To RecCount
         FileGet(Fnum, staff, n)
         If target = RTrim(staff.Dept) Then
            Display.Text &= staff.LName & " " & staff.Grade & " " &
staff.Hours & vbCrLf
         Finds = Finds + 1
         End If
      Next n
      If Finds = 0 Then
         MsgBox("No matching records", 48)
      Else
         Display.Text &= Finds & " Records"
      End If
End Sub
```

The **SelectGrade** sub is very similar. Copy and paste, then edit to create this code.

```
Private Sub SelectGrade_Click(ByVal sender As System.Object, ByVal e
As System.EventArgs) Handles SelectGrade.Click
   Dim target As Integer
   Dim Finds As Integer
   Dim n As Integer

   Display.Visible = True
   CloseBtn.Visible = True

   Finds = 0
   target = InputBox("Which Grade", "Select")
   Display.Text = "Grade:" & target & vbCrLf
   Display.Text = "Name               Department     Hours" & vbCrLf
   For n = 1 To RecCount
      FileGet(Fnum, staff, n)
      If target = staff.Grade Then
         Display.Text &= staff.LName & " " & staff.Dept & " " &
staff.Hours & vbCrLf
         Finds = Finds + 1
      End If
   Next n
   If Finds = 0 Then
      MsgBox("No matching records", 48)
   Else
      Display.Text &= Finds & " Records"
   End If
End Sub
```

12.8 Exercises

12.1 Working from the fragments given at the start of this chapter, write a program to handle student records, using a random access file for storage. The program should offer the same range of facilities as that in the staff database, plus routines to display total and average marks.

12.2 A pocket diary is a form of random access database, and one that can be implemented readily in Visual Basic. The functions that convert dates to numbers and vice versa, can be used to turn diary dates into record numbers, using statements like:

```
RecNo = DateValue(GivenDate) - DateValue("31/12/04")
```

This would produce record numbers for a 2004 diary. *GivenDate* must be in a suitable form and include the year number. As a similar expression can convert record numbers back into dates, you will not need to store dates in the records.

Appendix: Solutions to exercises

Chapter 3

3.1   As only one statement is conditional on each test, these can be written as single-line Ifs. The over 50,000 and below 20,000 tests are simple, but to spot the middle range you must test both limits, linking the two expressions with an AND.

```
Dim salary As Single
salary = InputBox("How much do you want to earn?")
If salary > 50000 Then MsgBox ("Don't go into writing")
If salary > 20000 And salary <= 50000 Then MsgBox ("Good luck")
If salary <= 20000 Then MsgBox ("What modest aims!")
```

3.2   The trick here is to make use of the fact that the end value in a **For ... Next** loop can be a variable. This gives us a link between the outer and inner loops.

```
Dim outer, inner As Integer
Output.Text = ""
For outer = 1 To 8
   For inner = 1 To outer
      Output.Text &= "*"
   Next inner
   Output.Text &= Chr(13) & Chr(10) ' start a new line
Next outer
```

3.4   This takes the member's age into a TextBox named *txtAge*, and displays the results in the Labels *lblCategory* and *lblFees*. The calculations are done in code attached to the Button *btnCheck*.

```
age = Val(txtAge.Text)
Select Case age
   Case 0 To 16
      lblCategory = "Junior"
      lblFees = "£125"
   Case 17 To 54
      lblCategory = "Adult"
      lblFees = "£250"
   Case 55 To 80
```

```
        lblCategory = "Senior"
        lblFees = "£125"
     Case Else
        lblCategory = "Honorary"
        lblFees = "Free"
End Select
```

4.1   Here, the code to check all five of the RadioButtons is written onto the Next Button's Click. An alternative would be to write checking code on each RadioButton.

Would this have made any difference to how the program was used?

A possible layout for the survey form.

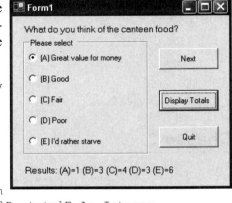

```
Public Class Form1
    Inherits System.Windows.Forms.Form
    Dim totalA, totalB, totalC, totalD, totalE As Integer
+ Windows Form Designer generated code
    Private Sub btnNext_Click(ByVal sender As System.Object, ByVal e
As System.EventArgs) Handles btnNext.Click
    If rdoA.Checked Then totalA += 1
    If rdoB.Checked Then totalB += 1
    If rdoC.Checked Then totalC += 1
    If rdoD.Checked Then totalD += 1
    If rdoE.Checked Then totalE += 1
    rdoA.Checked = True                    ' set the default
End Sub
    Private Sub btnDisplay_Click(ByVal sender As System.Object, ByVal
e As System.EventArgs) Handles btnDisplay.Click
    lblDisplay.Text = "Results: (A)=" & totalA & " (B)=" & totalB & "
(C)=" & totalC & " (D)=" & totalD & " (E)=" & totalE
End Sub
    Private Sub btnQuit_Click(ByVal sender As System.Object, ByVal e
As System.EventArgs) Handles btnQuit.Click
    End
End Sub
End Class
```

6.1   This has many possible solutions. The following makes a label, named *target*, appear at a random place on the form when the user clicks the Start Button. The starttime is recorded at this point. Code on the Click event of the target calculates the elapsed time and displays it on a label, named *lblFeedback*.

```
Public Class Form1
    Inherits System.Windows.Forms.Form
    Dim starttime, elapsed As Double
+ Windows Form Designer generated code
```

```
    Private Sub btnStart_Click(ByVal sender As System.Object, ByVal e
As System.EventArgs) Handles btnStart.Click
    starttime = Microsoft.VisualBasic.DateAndTime.Timer
    lblTarget.Top = Rnd() * 300
    lblTarget.Left = Rnd() * 400
    lblTarget.Visible = True
End Sub
    Private Sub lblTarget_Click(ByVal sender As System.Object, ByVal
e As System.EventArgs) Handles lblTarget.Click
    elapsed = Microsoft.VisualBasic.DateAndTime.Timer - starttime
    lblFeedback.Text = elapsed
End Sub
End Class
```

6.2   The simplest solution has a Label (here called *lblCounter*) that starts with a Caption of "10", and a Timer with its Interval set to 1000 – giving one-second intervals. The Timer can be enabled at design time or when the form loads. The code on the Timer should read:

```
    Private Sub Timer1_Tick(ByVal sender As System.Object, ByVal e As
System.EventArgs) Handles Timer1.Tick
        lblCounter.Text = Val(lblCounter.Text) - 1
        If lblCounter.Text = "0" Then Timer1.Enabled = False
    End Sub
```

7.2   There are three stages to this. First we go through the input phrase, copying the letters – but nothing else – into a new string (palindromes ignore spaces and punctuation). Then we run backwards though that string, copying the letter to build up a second string. Finally we compare the two strings and if they match, assign *True* to *palindrome*.

```
Private Function palindrome(ByVal s As String) As Boolean
    Dim s1, s2 As String
    Dim slength As Short = Len(s)
    Dim n As Short
    s = LCase(s)
    s1 = ""
    For n = 1 To slength
        If Mid(s, n, 1) >= "a" And Mid(s, n, 1) <= "z" Then
            s1 &= Mid(s, n, 1)
        End If
    Next
    s2 = ""
    For n = Len(s1) To 1 Step -1
        s2 &= Mid(s1, n, 1)
    Next
    If s2 = s1 Then palindrome = True Else palindrome = False
End Function
```

7.3   This relies on the fact that the ASCII code is numeric, so that you can calculate with its values. It uses the functions `Asc()` to convert a character into an ASCII number, and `Chr()` to convert an ASCII value back into a character. Here's the `encode()` sub.

The decode() sub is the same except that it subtracts the *key* value.

```
Private Sub encode()
   Dim count As Short
   Dim temp As String
   Dim key As Short
   key = InputBox("Code number")
   temp = TextArea.Text
   For count = 1 To Len(temp)
      Mid(temp, count, 1) = Chr(Asc(Mid(temp, count, 1)) + key)
   Next
   TextArea.Text = temp
End Sub
```

8.2 In my solution, I've used ScrollBars to set the colours, but the ColorDialog would work just as well – and take less code! Much of the code is straightforward, and I've omitted routines that are obvious. The most complex part is that which changes the colour in steady increments – notice that the change amounts are stored in Single variables, so that there can be fractional adjustments to the (Short) colour levels.

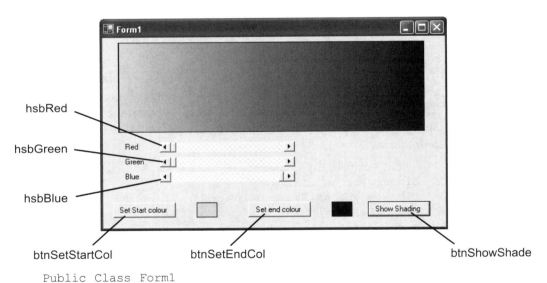

```
Public Class Form1
   Inherits System.Windows.Forms.Form
   Dim red, green, blue As Short
   Dim startRed, endRed, startGreen, endGreen, startBlue, endBlue As
Short
Windows Form Designer generated code
   Private Sub hsbRed_Scroll(ByVal sender As System.Object, ByVal e
As System.Windows.Forms.ScrollEventArgs) Handles hsbRed.Scroll
      red = hsbRed.Value
      picCanvas.BackColor = Color.FromArgb(red, green, blue)
   End Sub
' follow the same pattern for green and blue
   Private Sub btnSetStartCol_Click(ByVal sender As System.Object,
```

```
                  ByVal e As System.EventArgs) Handles btnSetStartCol.Click
        lblStart.BackColor = Color.FromArgb(red, green, blue)
        startRed = red
        startGreen = green
        startBlue = blue
    End Sub
    ' follow the same pattern for the end colour
        Private  Sub  btnShowShade_Click(ByVal  sender  As  System.Object,
    ByVal e As System.EventArgs) Handles btnShowShade.Click
        Dim bars As Short = picCanvas.Width
        Dim height As Short = picCanvas.Height
        Dim count As Short
        Dim redChange, greenChange, bluechange As Single
        Dim thisRed, thisGreen, thisBlue As Short
        Dim canvas As System.Drawing.Graphics = picCanvas.CreateGraphics
        Dim myPen As New Pen(Color.Black, 1)

        redChange = (endRed - startRed) / bars
        greenChange = (endGreen - startGreen) / bars
        bluechange = (endBlue - startBlue) / bars

        For count = 1 To bars
            thisRed = startRed + count * redChange
            thisGreen = startGreen + count * greenChange
            thisBlue = startBlue + count * bluechange
            myPen.Color = Color.FromArgb(thisRed, thisGreen, thisBlue)
            canvas.DrawLine(myPen, count, 0, count, height)
        Next
    End Sub
End Class
```

9.1   This solution uses four buttons are named *btnDisplay*, *btnEdit*, *btnMinMax* and *btnSort*, and a TextBox named *txtOuput*. Inputs are taking through InputBoxes.

```
    Private Sub btnDisplay_Click(ByVal sender As System.Object, ByVal
e As System.EventArgs) Handles btnDisplay.Click
    Dim n As Integer
    txtOutput.Text = ""
    For n = 0 To 9
        txtOutput.Text &= n & "   " & dataset(n) & vbCrLf
    Next n
End Sub

    Private Sub btnEdit_Click(ByVal sender As System.Object, ByVal e
As System.EventArgs) Handles btnEdit.Click
    Dim element As Integer
    element = InputBox("Enter item number")
    dataset(element) = InputBox("New value for item " & element)
End Sub

    Private Sub btnMinMax_Click(ByVal sender As System.Object, ByVal
e As System.EventArgs) Handles btnMinMax.Click
    Dim n As Integer
```

```
      Dim Min As Single, Max As Single
      Min = dataset(0)                        ' starting values
      Max = dataset(0)
      For n = 1 To 9
         If dataset(n) < Min Then Min = dataset(n)    ' found smaller
         If dataset(n) > Max Then Max = dataset(n)    ' found larger
      Next n
      MsgBox("Minimum = " & Min & vbCrLf & "Maximum = " & Max)
   End Sub
      Private Sub btnSort_Click(ByVal sender As System.Object, ByVal e
   As System.EventArgs) Handles btnSort.Click
      Dim n As Integer
      Dim temp As Single
      Dim sorted
      Do
         sorted = True
         For n = 0 To 8
            If dataset(n) > dataset(n + 1) Then
               temp = dataset(n)
               dataset(n) = dataset(n + 1)
               dataset(n + 1) = temp
               sorted = False
            End If
         Next n
      Loop Until sorted
   End Sub
```

9.2 If you know how many bars there are and how big they are, drawing a chart is very simple. It gets a bit trickier if you want a routine that can cope with any number of bars and any size of data – which is what we have here.

The number of bars determines their width and spacing. Here are the relevant lines – and note that these assume a 500 pixel wide chart area, and a slim gap between the bars.

```
   spacing = (500 / howmany)
   barwidth = spacing * 0.9     ' 90% of available width per bar
```

To ensure that the highest bar fits in the available space – and that the rest are all to scale, we need to find the height of the highest bar, then calculate a scale factor. My chart area is 300 pixels high.

```
   max = 0
   For n = 0 To howmany - 1
      If data(n) > max Then max = data(n)
   Next
   scale = 300 / max
```

The bars are drawn with FillRectangle(brush, x, y, width, height) where x and y locate the top left corner of the block. The x value is simply a multiple of the spacing value;

the y value is found by scaling the data item, then subtracting it from 300 – or whatever the height of your chart area may be:

```
x = n * spacing
y = 300 - data(n) * scale
```

Here's the whole drawing routine. It assumes that you have collected *howmany* data items in the *data()* array.

```
    Private Sub btnChart_Click(ByVal sender As System.Object, ByVal e
As System.EventArgs) Handles btnChart.Click
    Dim barwidth, spacing, max, scale As Single
    Dim n As Short
    Dim x, y, height As Single
    Dim chartarea As System.Drawing.Graphics = picChart.CreateGraphics
    Dim redBrush As New SolidBrush(Color.Red)
    Dim greenBrush As New SolidBrush(Color.Green)

    ' find bar width and spacing
    spacing = (500 / howmany)
    barwidth = spacing * 0.9     ' 90% of available width per bar
    ' find height and scale factor
    max = 0
    For n = 0 To howmany - 1
       If data(n) > max Then max = data(n)
    Next
    scale = 300 / max               ' the tallest bar will reach the top
    For n = 0 To howmany - 1
       x = n * spacing
       y = 300 - data(n) * scale
       height= data(n) * scale
       If n Mod 2 = 0 Then
          chartarea.FillRectangle(redBrush, x, y, barwidth, height)
       Else
          chartarea.FillRectangle(greenBrush, x, y, barwidth, height)
       End If
    Next
End Sub
```

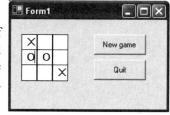

9.3   For the screen display of the board I have used a set of TextBoxes called *box0* to *box8*, (with matching TabIndex properties). This is linked to an array called *box()* where moves are stored, and where the checks are made for a winning line.

The New Game button (*btnNew*) simply wipes the board and the array, and initialises the *status* variable, which will later hold the results of checking the lines.

A single procedure handles the TextChanged events for all the TextBoxes, using `sender.tabindex` to identify the box and `sender.text` to identify the move. The checking routine sliced off into a separate procedure called *checkboard*.

The boxes are arranged with the index numbers in this pattern:

```
0   1   2
3   4   5
6   7   8
```

The calculations in the code flow from that. To check the rows, we start from boxes 0, 3 and 6, and compare them with the boxes numbered +1 and +2. To check the columns, we start at 0, 1 and 2 and compare their contents with those numbered +3 and +6. For the diagonals, we need to check the two sets 0, 4, 8 and 2, 4, 6.

The final check is for a full board, and that is just a matter of running through all the boxes to see if any are still empty. It's a crude system, and cannot spot the stalemates that can arise by move 7 or 8.

```
Public Class Form1
   Inherits  System.Windows.Forms.Form
   Dim status As Short
   Dim full As Boolean
   Dim box(9) As Short
+ Windows Form Designer generated code
   Private Sub btnNew_Click(ByVal sender As System.Object, ByVal e As
System.EventArgs)  Handles  btnNew.Click
   Dim n As Short
   status = 3                    ' initialising - do nothing at TextChanged
   box0.Text = ""
   box1.Text = ""
   box2.Text = ""
   box3.Text = ""
   box4.Text = ""
   box5.Text = ""
   box6.Text = ""
   box7.Text = ""
   box8.Text = ""
   For n = 0 To 8
      box(n) = 0
   Next
   status = 0
End Sub
   Private Sub box_TextChanged(ByVal sender As System.Object, ByVal
e As System.EventArgs)  Handles box0.TextChanged,  box1.TextChanged,
box2.TextChanged, box3.TextChanged, box4.TextChanged, box5.TextChanged,
box6.TextChanged,  box7.TextChanged,  box8.TextChanged
   If status = 3 Then Exit Sub              ' initialising
   Dim index As Short = sender.tabindex     ' which box?
   Dim marker As Char = sender.text         ' X or O
   If marker = "X" Then box(index) = 1 Else box(index) = 2
   checkboard()
End Sub
Private Sub checkboard()
   Dim row, col, n As Short
```

```
    For row = 0 To 6 Step 3          ' check rows
      If box(row) <> 0 Then          ' leftmost box not empty
         If box(row) = box(row + 1) And box(row) = box(row + 2) Then
            status = 1
         End If
      End If
   Next row
   For col = 0 To 2      ' check columns
      If box(col) <> 0 Then      ' topmost box not empty
         If box(col) = box(col + 3) And box(col) = box(col + 6) Then
            status = 1
         End If
      End If
   Next col
      ' check diagonals
      If box(4) <> 0 Then           ' centre box not empty
         If box(0) = box(4) And box(0) = box(8) Then
            status = 1
         End If
         If box(2) = box(4) And box(2) = box(6) Then
            status = 1
         End If
      End If
      ' check for full board
      full = True
      For n = 0 To 8
         If box(n) = 0 Then full = False
      Next n
      If full Then status = 2
      If status = 1 Then MsgBox("The Winner")
      If status = 2 Then MsgBox("It's a draw")
   End Sub
   Private Sub btnQuit_Click(ByVal sender As System.Object, ByVal e
As System.EventArgs) Handles btnQuit.Click
   End
End Sub
End Class
```

11.1   The main problem here is in transferring the data from the file to the Text of the RadioButtons and the question Label, as you cannot Input into them. The solution is to take the data via a temporary variable. The right answer, which will be held in a variable, can be Input directly. The code should then follow this pattern:

```
If EOF(1) Then Exit Sub
Input(1, temp)
lblQuestion.Text = temp
Input(1, temp)
rdoOpt1.Text = temp
...
Input(1, answer)
lblResult = ""
```

Note, that for this to work, the file must have been opened already (as 1) – perhaps by the **Form_Load** procedure.

For checking the answers, the simplest approach is to write "1", "2" or "3", to match the correct Option number, into the file. The result can then be shown when the user clicks an Option. This code could end with a line to call up the next question, and update a variable to keep track of the score.

```
Sub rdoOpt1_CheckChanged(...
   If answer = "1" Then
      lblResult = "Correct"
   Else
      lblResult = "Wrong"
   End If
End Sub
```

Index